Business Writing

Also in the Orion Business Toolkit Series

Effective Presentation by Sarah Dickinson
Marketing for Managers by David Mercer
People Management by Rosemary Thomson
NLP and the New Manager by Ian McDermott and Ian Shircore
Mastering the Internet by Ian Shircore and Richard Lander
Communicating With Customers by Patrick Forsyth
Profitable Negotiation by Gavin Kennedy
Effective Coaching by Myles Downey

Business Writing

Rupert Morris and Harriet Smith

➡ Orion Business Toolkit

ORION BUSINESS BOOKS

Copyright © 1999 by Rupert Morris and Harriet Smith

All rights reserved

The right of Rupert Morris and Harriet Smith to be identified
as the authors of this work has been asserted by them in accordance
with the Copyright, Designs and Patents Act 1988

First published in Great Britain in 1999 by
Orion Business
An imprint of The Orion Publishing Group Ltd
Orion House, 5 Upper St Martin's Lane, London WC2H 9EA

A CIP catalogue record for this book
is available from the British Library

ISBN 0-75282-077-X

Typeset by Deltatype Ltd, Birkenhead, Merseyside
Printed and bound in Great Britain by
Clays Ltd, St Ives plc

Contents

Introduction 1

Part 1 The writer's toolbox 3

    1 Assessing the job 5
- What is the message? 6
- Who is going to read this? 7

    2 Arranging the words – grammar 10
- Constructing sentences 10
- Writing positively 12
- Avoiding howlers 16

    3 Listening to the words – punctuation 22
- Why we punctuate 23
- The elements of punctuation 24

    4 Looking at the words – layout 33
- Varying layout with the type of document 37
- Summary 42

Part 2 Writing for results 45

- **5 What's the form?** 47
  - ➡ Opening moves 48
  - ➡ Signing off 52
  - ➡ Summary 53

- **6 Writing that works** 54
  - ➡ Applications and requests 54
  - ➡ Complaints and apologies 59
  - ➡ Introductions and references 63
  - ➡ Dismissal, rejection and resignation letters 67
  - ➡ Explanations and clarifications 72

- **7 Writing that sells** 74
  - ➡ Selling your services 75
  - ➡ Advertising your wares 78
  - ➡ Job applications 81
  - ➡ Invitations 82
  - ➡ Direct mailshots 85
  - ➡ Your aim in marketing 88

- **8 Organising your writing** 89
  - ➡ Listing items 89
  - ➡ Writing reports 91

- **9 Electronic mail** 102
  - ➡ Why use electronic mail? 102
  - ➡ Creating an e-mail message 103
  - ➡ Writing effective e-mail 106
  - ➡ The perils of e-mail 110

- **10 Corporate Writing Disease** 111
  - ➡ Waffle – tautology and verbosity 114
  - ➡ Nounitis 116
  - ➡ Exaggerations 117
  - ➡ Jargon 118
  - ➡ Summary 120

- **11 Summary and conclusions** 121

Index 133

Introduction

Why should anyone make a special effort to improve their writing? If you are not a particularly good writer, does it really matter? Yes, it does, and here's why:

- Words are often the first impression a customer has of a business.
- Whether it's a letter, e-mail message or detailed report, the style and quality of the writing presents the image of that business.
- Clear writing gets messages across effectively, whereas sloppy writing causes confusion, wastes time, and costs money.
- Effective writing brings results, whereas defensive writing merely causes problems to pile up.
- You can't avoid writing altogether, can you?

Research shows that successful companies are good communicators. Their literature is clear and simple. The language they use is accessible to all. Their staff know how to write well. Why? It's very straightforward. When you are thinking clearly, and you have good messages to convey, communication is a pleasure. But when you are directionless, lacking in motivation, and having nothing positive to say, you naturally become defensive and evasive.

So, written material – whether letters, memos, e-mails or reports – is bound to present the image of the business to the outside world. Well written literature gives an impression of competence and instils confidence in the reader; evasive, officious writing puts people off. Nobody wants to receive written communications that are incomprehensible, irrelevant or a struggle to read.

Why, then, are so many people involved in business unable to write well? More important, what can be done to remedy the situation?

Writing well requires effort. The French philosopher Blaise Pascal once wrote to a friend and apologised for having written such a long letter. 'I didn't have time to write a short one,' he explained. The more you write, the more you realise that the most precious skill of all is to be able to cut out all irrelevant or tangential material and give your reader the clearest, most concise message possible.

For busy people with little free time, this book will help you to develop a clear, concise writing style that will enhance your market value. It will teach you the essential tricks of the trade and help you to approach everyday problems in a calmer, more analytical and purposeful way. The chapters cover every kind of writing, from memos and press releases to major reports.

Business Writing is not a text book, but a practical manual, which can be read as a whole or used as a resource to which you can return again and again for advice on specific areas. Part 1, 'The writer's toolbox', starts with the essential tools of writing – grammar, punctuation and lay-out – and shows you how to use them to communicate effectively. Part 2, 'Writing for results', relates the writing to the messages you wish to convey, and shows you how to have the desired effect on your readership in many different situations.

Part 1
The writer's toolbox

Chapter 1
Assessing the job

Before we look in detail at grammar and punctuation, it is vital to bear this in mind: in business writing, your object should always be to boil a subject down to its essentials. Ask yourself some of these questions:

- What really matters here?
- What am I trying to achieve?
- What is the best way of getting the message to this particular reader?
- What will they think or feel when they read this?
- Will I get the result I want?

We have called this part of the book 'The writer's toolbox', and it makes sense that you assess the job in hand before you get the tools out.

Here is an example of how not to do it. A management training company has just outlined the purpose of its new programme, and is about to go into greater detail. Its brochure says: 'The information that follows will provide you with an in-depth look at its process and content.' The whole point of this sentence is to make the reader read on. But the writer is so desperate to make everything sound important that he feels obliged to offer 'an in-depth look at its process and content'. This sort of flannel merely slows the reader down, making the whole thing sound more complicated and less inviting.

That sentence should simply say: 'Here's how it works' – fewer words, swifter communication, and more chance that the reader actually will read on. Please note: no literary skill is required, just a clear sense of purpose.

➡ WHAT IS THE MESSAGE?

The key to good communication is putting the main message up front. There is no point in advertising a new brand of shampoo with loads of information about how good it is for you if the special offer is lost in the bottom right-hand corner. Wave the information in the public's face!

> **FOUR FOR THE PRICE OF ONE:**
> **massive savings on own-brand shampoo!!!!!!!!**

The rest of the message is relatively unimportant.

The same applies to longer pieces of writing. Always start with what you really want to get across. For instance:

> 'One of the secrets of successful investing is not just choosing the right stocks, but avoiding the wrong ones', writes James Gardner in *Investor's Monthly*.

Having made its point clearly, the article goes on to explain why. Readers know exactly what they will be reading about.

And here is a useful tip: read the professionals. Reporters are trained to write news stories in descending order of importance. The headline draws your attention and tells you as much as it can. The first paragraph tries to give you the story in a nutshell. The second and third paragraphs provide the most important additional information; and so on, in declining importance down the page, so that readers know what has happened even if they do not finish the whole article.

This is a skill that applies to every type of writing. It doesn't matter whether it is a memo or an annual report – the focus of any document should be on the core message.

Even something as simple as leaving a note on someone's desk can go wrong if the message isn't clear enough. Compare the following memos intended to pass on an important phone call:

MEMO A

> Wendy,
> That chap you met at the BA do last week rang. I think he might be interested in doing business. Please will you phone him back asap?
> 01111 111 111
> John

MEMO B

> *Wendy,*
> *I've just had to rush out for half-an-hour – an urgent call from one of my clients who isn't very happy with our ideas. I can't imagine why – I thought the storyboards were very good. Never mind, I'm sure I'll sort him out. See you later. Oh, some chap you met last week rang. Think he wanted you to ring him.*
> *John*

Obviously the first message is the one that will succeed. The second one completely fails to get across the urgency of the phone call, and omits the vital number. All too often, busy people do not take the time to step back and think about the impact of their words by asking themselves such questions as:

- Am I getting the message across clearly?
- Will they realise it's urgent?
- Do they need to know about my problems?

It only takes a moment to remember that the crucial part of the message is the caller's number, not the fact that the author of the message is in a flap. Which brings us to the next question:

➡ WHO IS GOING TO READ THIS?

No professional writer will ever embark on a report, speech or article without first asking who it is for. Nor should you. A speech that might win a standing ovation from an audience of policemen might elicit a very different reaction from, say, the inmates of Barlinnie Jail. And a report on workers' rights that would delight trades' unionists might well appal industrialists. Tailoring your words to your audience is not just a politician's trick. It's common sense.

So before you get that writer's toolbox out, just consider:

- Who are my likely readers?
- How will they view this subject?
- How can I get through to them?

In the memo we examined a moment ago, the writer knew that the audience was Wendy, the person receiving the message. But in the second version, he had completely forgotten Wendy, and was really writing, without thinking, for himself.

Not only do you need to know who your readers are; you also need to have a good idea how they will react. Experience may give you the answer, or you may have to use your imagination. Put yourself into their shoes. How would *you* feel if you received the letter, report or memo in question? Would you understand it? Does it speak your language? It's amazing how often business communications completely fail to use the reader's language – and officious language is a particularly common problem.

The following example demonstrates how not to treat an audience. The subject is a pet's insurance policy:

VERSION A

Failure to disclose all material facts which have changed since inception or last renewal of your policy could result in your insurance being invalidated. Material facts are those facts which might influence the acceptance or assessment of your insurance. If you are in any doubt as to whether a fact is material you should declare it.

It is easy to see how this convoluted paragraph crept into the policy. The company will have taken legal advice on how to ensure that they are aware of any changes in the policyholder's circumstances that might affect their coverage. The problem is that they did not think beyond the legalese to the reaction of the customer. To many people, the paragraph will come across as bewildering gobbledegook and could cause them to worry. It would have been much simpler to write:

VERSION B

> Please tell us if there have been any changes in your pet's circumstances since you took out the policy. For instance, has your animal had a serious illness or accident? If you do not let us know, your policy may no longer be valid.

Starting with 'please' is much less intimidating than 'failure'. 'Material facts' could mean anything, including issues that have nothing to do with the pet's insurance. 'Inception' is an unnecessarily officious word. It's not so hard to explain the matter in everyday language. Readers need to know what the company wants, and what they must do to comply.

Now that we know our purpose, our message and our reader(s), it's time to get the toolbox out.

Chapter 2
Arranging the words – grammar

Learning to write is like learning to cook. You can't do either unless you know a few basic rules. If you wanted to bake a cake, for example, you would need a baking tin and greaseproof paper, a list of the basic ingredients (butter, sugar, flour, eggs, milk, salt, dried fruit, brandy), the quantities of each, instructions on how to mix the ingredients, and an oven, with instructions on settings and timings. If you don't have this information, you won't be able to bake the cake. Knowing the ingredients but not the quantities, or knowing both of these, but not the order in which the ingredients are mixed, will almost certainly result in a soggy, unappealing mess – which is just how a lot of business writing turns out.

The writer's equivalent of a recipe is grammar and punctuation – words that strike horror into those of us who struggled with the rules at school. Don't be disheartened – it isn't nearly as complicated as it seems; in fact, it's as easy as baking a cake.

➡ CONSTRUCTING SENTENCES

The basis of all writing is the sentence, a complete statement that can stand by itself. Grammar is simply a matter of putting the words of the sentence in the right order. You can write without a basic understanding of grammar, but you won't write well. And you won't know how to correct a sentence if it goes horribly wrong, just as a cook without the basic knowledge can't rescue a cake.

Sentences are the backbone of good writing. Most experts agree that clear writing has an average sentence length of between 15 and 25 words. This doesn't mean that you have to make every sentence the same length, but staying close to that number makes life easier for the reader.

Use your imagination. Write short punchy sentences. Then vary the text with longer, more descriptive ones. Try to keep the language simple and clear. Many writers try to say too much in one sentence:

> *The question of you receiving a further grant will be at the Trust's discretion and if you are indeed accepted for another grant you will be informed and if you are successful you may apply for a further grant for the following year.*

By the end of this sentence, you have to go back to the beginning to remember how it started. The sense is much clearer if it is broken down into shorter sentences:

> The Trust will decide whether or not you receive a further grant for this year. If you are successful, we will inform you as soon as possible. You may then apply for another grant for next year.

Looks easy, doesn't it? And it can be, particularly if you stick to a sound structure.

Sentence structure

Sentences consist of a number of individual elements, of which the main ones are: the subject (the doer), the verb (the activity) and the object (the done-to).

'The dog (subject) bit (verb) the postman (object).' or
'Your uncle (subject) forgot (verb) his umbrella (object).'

It is also possible to have a sentence without an object – the most famous one is 'Jesus wept' – but it is unusual.

There is no law that says that the subject, verb and object have to be in this order (see example overleaf) but it helps to understand their role. Choosing the right subject for the sentence is vital.

Consider this sentence from a brochure produced by Scottish lawyers for English clients:

As lawyers in Scotland we are not often recognised as estate agents, although the law is different, by English clients.

This is a horribly disjointed sentence. It is hard to work out which part belongs to which. But use a different subject, and it becomes much clearer:

English clients are often unaware that Scottish lawyers can act as estate agents [because of the different legal system].

Some technical terms

In discussing grammar, we have to use certain technical terms. The two most important are nouns (things or people) and verbs (doing words). The subject or object of a sentence has to be a noun or a pronoun (which is a word that stands in for a noun, such as 'I', 'you', 'he', 'it' or 'them').

We also have adjectives (words that qualify nouns, such as 'good', 'bad', 'early', 'short' etc) and adverbs (words that qualify verbs, such as 'quickly', 'sharply', 'suddenly', 'easily'). Then we have conjunctions (short linking words such as 'and', 'but', 'since' and 'because' and prepositions (linking words that express movement, such as 'to', 'from', 'under', 'beyond'). Finally, we have the definite article ('the') and the indefinite article ('a').

These are our basic tools. Now let's look at how best to use them.

➡ WRITING POSITIVELY

Good writing should be active. You should use positive words that suggest action, and make sure real people are involved. Try, whenever possible to use words like 'we', 'you' and 'they', rather than 'the company' 'the insured' or 'the bank'. This is because the company or business is a faceless institution to which most people can't relate; 'we', instead of 'company' gives the reader a sense of belonging. It also helps enormously in sentence construction.

ARRANGING THE WORDS – GRAMMAR

Good grammar is not a complicated matter. On the contrary, it is all about making things simpler. If you want to communicate, you want to help the reader. Take this sentence, about the work of the Natural Environment Research Council:

> *From a growing scientific understanding of the Earth's processes, the links between them and the impact of man's activities, the NERC gives advice both on exploiting the natural resources of the land and sea and on protecting the world's environment.*

Quite a mouthful. The sentence seems starved of oxygen. Let's break it up and reform it:

> We need to understand life on earth and how human actions affect the natural systems around us. That is why the NERC advises on how to exploit the natural resources of land and sea, while protecting the environment.

If we break down into grammatical terms these two versions of the same message, we can see what was wrong with the first version. That single sentence has a total of 14 nouns and only three verbs – a ratio of nearly five to one. There are eight nouns before we get to the first verb. This is very unhealthy.

Now look at the improved version. The number of nouns has been reduced to nine, and there are seven verbs. Verbs, we know, are doing words, and they make your writing come alive. So use more verbs, and get things moving.

Active versus passive

The passive voice has nothing to do with the past tense. It is just a way of turning a sentence round, e.g.

> This issue will be addressed shortly. (Passive)
> We will address this matter shortly. (Active)

The passive voice shifts the emphasis onto the situation rather than the individuals concerned. This is fair enough in certain instances. But just look at the examples above, and there is an important difference: in the passive version, we don't say who is going to address the issue. We avoid responsibility – and that is what people are doing most of the time when they use the passive.

Using the passive thus tends to keep readers at a distance. Consider these examples and note how the tone and impression change when expressed in the active voice:

PASSIVE	ACTIVE
You will be notified in writing.	I'll write to you.
You will be collected at the airport.	We'll pick you up.

Using the active voice makes the reader feel there is a real person behind the letter and not some corporate bureaucracy.

The passive can be useful, however, when you want to emphasise the *what* and gloss over the *whom*. For instance:

> Your proposal was carefully considered but, in the end, it was felt that this would not be an appropriate course of action.

In this case, the identity of the person who actually considered and rejected the proposal isn't important; what matters is the decision that was made.

Clearly, vague vocabulary and the passive voice are very useful if you want to keep things unclear, evade responsibility and avoid being tied down by your words. But if this becomes a habit in written business communications, you will soon appear wishy-washy, confused, half-hearted and totally lacking in commitment, clarity, organisation and control. Compare the following:

PASSIVE	ACTIVE
The decision was made.	I made the decision.
It was decided.	We decided.

Using the active voice conveys the impression that the writer has control of the situation and also establishes a human connection between the writer and the reader. It shows that the writer is prepared to take responsibility.

Aim to make about 80–90 per cent of your verbs active. If you work on a PC, you can make sure by running your work through the grammar checker.

Abstractions

Another technique for evasive writers is to use 'abstract' nouns, which are not physical objects but concepts or ideas. They are often formed from verbs, and corporate writers use them far too often. Examples include: 'completion', 'introduction', 'provision', 'arrangement', 'function', 'level' and 'facility'.

Too many of these make writing stodgy and dull. Compare the following examples:

> *If you would like consideration to be given to your application for housing benefit, please send in your rent book.*

This immediately puts the reader at arm's length from the housing benefit people, and makes the whole process impersonal. The sentence can be rewritten in a much more friendly way:

> We will consider your application for housing benefit when you send us your rent book.

The use of the verb 'consider' and the pronoun 'we' makes it more positive, and encourages action on the claimant's part. Similarly:

> *Failure to inform us of any change to the completion date will result in immediate penalties.*

can be rewritten in a clearer and more direct style as:

> Please let us know if you cannot complete on the agreed date. By missing the deadline you may incur immediate penalties.

Abstract nouns and passive constructions not only put the reader at a distance; they result in unnecessarily long-winded sentences that often make little sense.

Read through something that you have recently written for work. If it seems distant and formal, you may have succumbed to nounitis (discussed at greater length in Chapter 10). See if you can take out some of the nouns, insert the odd verb and speed up the whole sentence.

➡ AVOIDING HOWLERS

Howlers in grammar happen when writers become slapdash. The more common problems with grammar are highlighted below.

Subject/verb agreement

Failing to make the subject and verb agree is a classic example of a howler. The rule should be very simple: a singular subject takes a singular verb, and a plural subject takes a plural verb. For example:

> A rake (singular subject) is (singular verb) a useful implement.
> Rakes (plural) are (plural verb) useful implements.

But if you have a longer sentence, you can confuse the singular and plural.

> The use of rakes, spades, edging tools and shears makes all the difference to the look of a garden.

The subject of this sentence is 'the use', so the verb 'makes' is singular. But because it is followed by a series of plurals, there is a temptation to make the verb plural. This would be wrong, and it wouldn't make sense. The tools don't make the difference. It is the use of them that does.

A more common mistake is with collective nouns, such as 'team', 'group', 'association' or 'company'. Although each of these contains (note the singular verb here, because the subject is 'each, not 'these') many people, each one constitutes a single entity, and should take a singular verb. After all, you can have a team, and you can have teams (plural).

It is wrong, therefore, to write:

> The Local Government Association (singular noun) are (plural verb) introducing a new reporting system.

It may sound all right, but it should have read:

> The Local Government Association, *is* . . . (singular verb)

This is a problem area for business writers, because in everyday conversation, people constantly get it wrong ('The Council are coming to fix the drains;' 'The band have broken up'). So does it matter? In business it matters, not least because a company is a single legal entity. Companies like McBrambles Restaurants sound as if they ought to be plural, but they are not. The best way of dealing with this is to use 'we' and 'our' as soon as possible in communications. This personalises the contact and reduces the risk of going wrong. So you can start a letter by writing:

> McBrambles Restaurants (collective noun) is (singular verb) pleased that you have won our lucky dip.

You then go on to write:

> We (plural pronoun, meaning all the staff) look forward to seeing you again soon.

From then on 'we' (plural) becomes the subject, taking a plural verb.

It seems complicated, but with a bit of practice it becomes clear and leads us naturally on to pronouns.

Pronouns

Subject and object pronouns confused
A common mistake is to write: 'John and me will go' when it should be 'John and I will go'; or 'A letter arrived for my husband and I' when it should be 'A letter arrived for my husband and me.'

A sure way of getting the right answer is to take the other person out of the sentence. You wouldn't say 'me will go' or 'a letter arrived for I.'

Reflexive or intensive pronouns (those ending -self)
These pronouns have two specific purposes: either intensive, as in

'I did it myself' (meaning alone and without help) or reflexive as in 'He included himself in the team'. They should not be used in any other way.

Thus it is wrong to write:

Details must be sent from your bankers to ourselves.

It should instead be one of the following:

Details must be sent to us from your bankers.
Your bankers must send us your details.

Particularly horrible is the ingratiating 'If this is convenient to yourself...'

Possessive pronouns

A common mistake is to write:

I hated him smoking in the office.

when it should be

I hated his smoking in the office.

Why? Because it wasn't him I hated; it was his smoking.

Tenses

Tenses are about our relationship to time. *Is* something happening in the present? *Did* it happen in the past? *Will* it happen in the future?

Many writers mix up their tenses:

I believed (past tense) that I can (present tense) turn water into wine.

makes no sense. If you believed something in the past, then whatever you believed belongs in the past:

I believed that I was able (past) to turn water into wine.

ARRANGING THE WORDS – GRAMMAR

Whether or not you did manage to turn water into wine doesn't matter. If you still believe that you have miraculous powers, the sentence should read:

> I believe (present) that I can (present) turn water into wine.

Imagine yourself at the moment of writing. Are you writing about something that is happening? Something that is over and done with? Something that might be going to happen? Or even a mixture of all three? Ask yourself which applies before you actually start writing. In this way

> *I believed (past) that I will (future) be able to turn water into wine*

is a step too far, for it is not possible to use the past and future tenses in the same sentence. But you can use the conditional:

> I believed (past) that I could (conditional) turn water into wine.

You can move from the past to the present in a sentence by using the present perfect tense ('have done' something). The following incorrect example comes from a local Electoral Registration Authority:

> *If you are living at your present address since before 11 October last year then it is likely that you are registered for your present address.*

The present tense is inappropriate for an activity that may date back to 11 October last year. You need the present perfect, which places a past event in a present context:

> If you have been living at your present address since before 11 October last year, then you are probably listed at that address on the electoral roll.

Another common pitfall is to confuse the past with the present, as shown by the following example:

> *I was afraid that you have not understood what I meant.*

This is an uncomfortable sentence, and should read as either one or other of the following:

> I was afraid that you had not understood what I meant. (Everything in the past tense.)
> I am afraid that you have not understood what I meant. (Past events brought into the present.)

Thinking about tenses can become confusing. Don't worry about correctness. What matters most is that you try to put everything in a clear order for your reader's benefit. If you are in any doubt, read your sentences out loud to check the tenses. If the words sound wrong, you may have got them muddled. Just rewrite until you have something in which the order of events is clear.

Modifiers

A modifier is any part of a sentence that comes outside the subject–verb–object part (called a 'clause') but is related to it. In the following examples, the modifier is in bold type:

> **When the sun shines,** we go to the beach.
> The bus driver, **who has a very bad temper,** threw the hooligan off the bus.

The first sentence can be written the other way round as the modifier only relates to one other part of the sentence. But by moving the modifier in the second sentence, you can change the sense completely:

> The bus driver threw the hooligan, **who has a very bad temper,** off the bus.

Modifiers can cause havoc in sentences if they are put in the wrong place. Here is a famous example from a local newspaper report:

> *When Her Majesty had broken the traditional bottle of champagne over the bows of the ship, she slid slowly and gracefully down the slipway, entering the water with scarcely a splash.*

The following misplaced modifier is merely irritating:

As a confirmed bachelor, Sunshine Leisure Holidays invites you to join our summer sun fun.

This is wrong – wrong because it misleads the reader. It opens with 'As a confirmed bachelor...' and the reader expects the next words to describe who that confirmed bachelor is. The answer, apparently, is Sunshine Leisure Holidays – which makes no sense at all. The sentence should read:

Sunshine Leisure Holidays invites you, as a confirmed bachelor, to join our summer sun fun.

Or:

As you are a confirmed bachelor, you are invited to Sunshine Leisure Holidays' summer sun fun.

When you insert a modifier, or qualifying phrase, you should put it as close as possible to whatever it relates to. Be clear about what is the subject of the sentence. And remember: the subject of one sentence can often be read as the subject of the next – as this extract from a magazine article reminds us:

Apart from water, camels are the most valuable possession of the Bedouin. These days they wear trainers under their traditional Arab robes, get their food in tins from supermarkets, and play Gameboys and guitars, yet they cling tenaciously to simple values like their sense of community in which everything, including problems, are shared.

Above all, read it through!

Chapter 3
Listening to the words – punctuation

Writing is a form of conversation, a way of building a relationship. You don't speak in a level monotone; you modulate your words for the listener's benefit. You emphasise certain words, raise and lower your voice, and pause every now and then, either for emphasis, or simply to take a breath. You should write in the same way.

You can't see your reader, so you just have to imagine how they might react. Apart from the words you use and the length of your sentences, your main tool is punctuation. That's why we use commas, now and then, to break up our written conversation; semi-colons are useful, too, if we want slightly longer pauses. A new thought requires a full stop and a new sentence. We shall go into more detail in a moment.

Almost all the worst business writing is in a language that no one would ever use in real life. Writing should never be like that. It is part of real life. So please remember:

- Writing is a form of conversation.
- Think of your reader as if you were talking to them.
- Punctuate for expression.
- Play it back to yourself to check that it sounds right.

Let's check this out with a real-life example of a letter from a supermarket to a customer:

> *May I firstly say that I can fully appreciate the comments you have made. However, as I'm sure you can appreciate, as a major retailing*

> outlet, and due to the enormous quantity of eggs demanded by our customers, together with those which have to be incorporated in to our recipes, this does dictate that we must source our requirements from a variety of suppliers.

The whole paragraph is a terrible mouthful, pompous, verbose and unfriendly. The grammar is appalling: can you find the subject of the second sentence? Actually, it is the thirty-seventh word: 'this'. But there's a simpler way of ruling out such a paragraph. It just isn't something you would say to a customer. So let's start again, using conversational language:

> I appreciate the points you make. Nonetheless, we are a major retailer, and the sheer volume of eggs we require means that we have to use several different suppliers.

This works much better, not only because it consists of two straightforward sentences but also because it is everyday language, and the reader understands it at once.

If you find it hard to stop yourself writing in a starchy, officious way, just read out something you've written. Do your written words sound like something you would say? Does the language flow freely? Will it encourage the reader to respond? Are the words simple and direct? If the answer to these questions is 'No, my writing doesn't sound at all like my conversation', try rephrasing your words in your head until they sound more like the spoken word – as well as something you would want to read.

Of course not all writing wants to be quite as informal as an everyday conversation. But even long reports need to be written in a way that encourages the audience to read on.

➡ WHY WE PUNCTUATE

One of the devices used in conversation – usually unconsciously – is punctuation. It allows you to pause in the right place, time your phrases, and emphasise the key wording. It helps a sentence to flow up and down, gaining a rhythm that makes it more understandable. And it allows the speaker time to think ahead if necessary. Being able to punctuate is a very useful skill, yet many people are unaware that they have it. This is because they don't relate what they say to what they write.

Try saying the following sentence out loud:

> *If you could let me have the latest version of the Annual Report I'll take it home to read it over the weekend and let you know if I have any changes on Monday.*

By the time you get to 'weekend', you've run out of breath and the words sound very flat. In contrast:

> Please may I have the latest version of the Annual Report? I'll take it home to read over the weekend, and let you have any changes on Monday.

is what you would probably say. The ideas are the same and the words are almost identical, but the simple addition of a question mark and a comma have transformed the sentence from being breathless and difficult to follow into a straightforward request. In conversation, you would do it instinctively. Punctuation has the same effect on writing.

➡ ELEMENTS OF PUNCTUATION

Knowing how to punctuate is one of the most useful tools in the writer's kit, and can make the difference between a bad sentence and a good one. In the rest of this chapter, we look at the role of different forms of punctuation, or, as Fowler's *Modern English Usage* defines them, stops.

Full stop (.)

Everyone thinks they know about full stops. They end sentences, don't they? The problem comes when there aren't enough of them. Many writers of documents, particularly when they write on behalf of public bodies or insurance companies, forget that brevity is the soul of clarity.

The following letter, from a building society, contains a paragraph that is one sentence long:

> *Should you be unable to agree to the contents of the statement or you have any questions thereon, please write to this department at the address overleaf, enclosing your passbook or certificate and the statement.*

It reads much more easily if you add an extra full stop (and use friendly language):

> If you can't agree to the contents of the statement or have any questions on it, please write to us at the address over the page. Please enclose your passbook or certificate and the statement. [© Plain English Campaign]

If your sentences are long, try reading them out. You'll probably find yourself putting in a full stop automatically.

Another common mistake is to cram two sentences into one, as in this fax message:

> *It is of the utmost urgency that you help me in this matter, for many reasons I need to be back in America immediately.*

Without a full stop, the reader initially assumes that 'for many reasons' belongs with the first part of the sentence. Put a full stop in the middle and it's much easier to read.

> It is of the utmost urgency that you help me in this matter. For many reasons, I need to be back in America immediately.

Comma (,)

A comma is a pause for breath during a sentence. Use one when you wish to separate one phrase from another:

> Under the terms of the new Act, young offenders will be subject to curfew after 8 p.m.

The comma breaks up the sentence, and separates the Act from the young offenders.

Commas can also be used in place of brackets (parentheses), which are ugly, and clutter up the page:

> Sir John Smart, chairman of BG Enterprises, said last Saturday...

This comma separates the qualification from the main part of the sentence, which would otherwise read: Sir John Smart said last Saturday... The words between the commas merely provide additional information. The same principle is at work here:

> Twenty-three years after the flood, but only ten since the house blew down, David returned to his old home.

Commas are very useful for breaking up your writing. But they cannot take the place of full stops.

> *I do not seem to have the information required from you to set up your budget scheme, I now enclose the relevant form for you to complete and return.*

What is wrong with this? It is really two sentences, two separate thoughts. The first is an observation ('I do not seem to have...'); the second is an action ('I now enclose...'). A comma is not enough to separate the two thoughts. A semi-colon would just about do the job (see below), but a full stop would probably be best:

> I do not seem to have the information I need from you in order to set up your budget scheme. I now enclose the relevant form for you to complete and return.

There are times when the use of a comma can change the meaning of a sentence, so be careful how you use them:

> The trainees, who will join the scheme next week, are quick learners.

Here, the main information is that the trainees are quick learners, and the commas are working like brackets. Without the commas, the meaning is quite different:

The trainees who will join the scheme next week are quick learners.

Now we are talking only about the trainees who are to join the scheme next week. Whether the rest of the trainees are quick learners or not is anyone's guess.

If you are in doubt about whether and where to use commas, just say the sentence out loud, and work out how you want it to sound. Commas will give it a certain emphasis, and you have to decide whether that is the emphasis you want.

Colon (:)

Colons introduce:

- lists (like this one)
- quotations (Simon says: 'Put your hands on your head . . .')
- explanations ('There is one problem with cricket on the radio: you can't see the game.')

There are hundreds of colons scattered throughout this book – look at almost any page to see how and when they are used. A colon is not a full stop, so the word immediately afterwards will not normally start with a capital letter. The only exception is when you are using a colon to introduce a series of paragraphs, each containing several sentences. In such instances, if it would look ridiculous to begin each paragraph in lower case, then you should feel free to start with capital letters.

There was a time when colons were sometimes followed by a dash, like this:– but the dash never added anything, has now gone out of fashion completely, and is not acceptable to most publishers.

Semi-colon (;)

Semi-colons are sometimes confused with colons; they should not be, because they have an entirely different function. The difference is simply this: colons introduce; semi-colons separate.

A semi-colon is actually very much as it looks: half-way between a comma and a full stop. If you want a pause for breath that is longer than a comma, but not as decisive as a full stop, a semi-colon is just the job. Semi-colons usually separate stand-alone, but related sentences, like the one at the start of this section.

They can also be used to separate items in a list. Here is one example:

> Target audiences for the new manual will include: other companies in our group; business leaders; top politicians and opinion formers; consultants; local schools and colleges.

Here is another example:

> Among the guests were: Sir Richard Eyre, former director of the National Theatre; Anita Roddick, founder of The Body Shop; Sebastian Faulks, author of *Birdsong*; and Gillon Aitken, the literary agent.

If you were just listing the names, commas would do, but when each one has a brief qualification, you need semi-colons.

Dash (–)

The dash has become an accepted form of punctuation, although there was a time not so long ago when it was looked on as slovenly. Some people use too many; others hardly use them at all, and so this is largely a matter of personal preference.

You can use a dash instead of a comma if you want a longer pause:

> He gambled on the money markets for pleasure – and because he was greedy.

A comma wouldn't have worked here as the emphasis needs to be on 'greedy', not 'pleasure'. The dash allows a more dramatic pause.

Dashes can also be used instead of brackets when you want to insert a brief idea in a sentence:

> There are various times of day – particularly after meals – when most of us lose energy and tend to feel sleepy.

Avoid using dashes and hyphens too close together.

Hyphen (-)

Hyphens – not to be confused with dashes like these – link adjectives that carry equal weight and that qualify a noun. So 'part-time employee' has the front portion hyphenated because both 'part' and 'time' are acting as a single adjective to describe the noun 'employee'. The following are only a few of hundreds of examples: 'computer-based work', 'high-cost strategy', 'long-term view', 'state-of-the-art equipment', 'reply-paid forms'.

There are also a few nouns that are formed by two words and that need the hyphen to make their meaning clear: 'hang-up', 'stand-by', 'lean-to', 'grown-up', 'run-up', etc.

Inverted commas (' ', " ")

Most people use inverted commas for quotations, and there is no set rule about whether or not to use single or double marks. The tendency seems to be for reported speech to be in double quotes:

"The Lady's not for turning," declared Margaret Thatcher in 1981.

Some people prefer to use single inverted commas, and only use double inverted commas when there is a quotation within a quotation. This is the preferred style used by UK book publishers, but in practice, it doesn't matter which way round you use them as long as the sense is clear.

Inverted commas can also be used within a sentence to distinguish titles, phrases or technical terms, such as 'electronic mail', Jack 'the Hat' McVitie, etc. However, they should not be used otherwise to differentiate words for no specific reason, as here:

I was 'green' with envy.

The word 'green' is being used metaphorically, but this is common enough usage not to require inverted commas, which merely draw unnecessary attention to the word and interrupt the flow of the whole sentence.

Above all, putting anything in inverted commas implies: 'These are not my words.' This prompts the obvious question: so why use them? Why not say what you really mean?

Punctuation within inverted commas can cause problems. Normally, the test is whether the punctuation belongs within the inverted commas or not. In this case, for instance, it is easy:

Ron said: 'I'm not coming.'

Simple enough. What Ron said was a sentence in itself. But if you turned it round, the punctuation within the inverted commas would change:

'I'm not coming,' said Ron.

If there is a narrative continuing after the quotation, punctuation is usually tucked inside the inverted commas, even if it doesn't belong to the sentence within the inverted commas:

'The problem,' said Ron, 'is that I can't really afford to come.'

Apostrophe (')

Apostrophes have two main uses.

The first is to indicate possession by replacing the word 'of'. If you are unsure about when to use an apostrophe, try reinserting the 'of'. For example: 'The dog's collar' indicates the collar of the dog; 'the bank's employees' describes the employees of the bank.

Problems often arise when you have to decide if the apostrophe should go before or after the 's'. If the noun is plural, the apostrophe should always go after. Imagine that you are writing about company executives and their wives. Is it 'the company executive's wives' or 'the company executives' wives'? The latter must apply, because if you reinsert the 'of', you realise that it must be the wives of the executives (plural). Otherwise, someone would be a bigamist!

Names that end in 's' can also cause problems in this area. Do you write 'Mrs Bloggs' newspaper' or 'Mrs Bloggs's newspaper'? Either would be correct, but the best test is what you would actually say. If you say "Mrs Bloggs's newspaper", pronouncing both esses, then write it that way.

The second use is to indicate a missing letter, as in 'don't' (do not), 'can't' (cannot) or 'won't' (will not), or to stand for missing numbers, as in '98 instead of 1998.

Never put an apostrophe in the possessive pronouns 'his', hers', 'its', 'theirs' 'ours' or 'yours'. 'It's' (with an apostrophe) is an abbreviated form of 'it is'. If you tend to confuse this with the possessive its, just remember this sentence:

> It's a good dog that knows its master.

You know that the first instance stands for 'it is', and therefore must have the apostrophe; the second instance is the possessive, and must be different – no apostrophe.

Question mark (?)

If a sentence is a question, it should end in a question mark. There is no need to add any other punctuation after the question mark.

If a sentence contains a reported question, there is no need to use a question mark as the sentence is in fact a statement:

> I asked him to tell me when he was going home.

Exclamation mark (!)

These are used to follow exclamations of surprise, shock or dismay. Only use one at a time – '!!!' looks absurd on the written page. And don't use them to indicate a witticism or a clever remark – if it's witty enough, readers should be able to work it out for themselves.

Brackets (( ))

Brackets, like inverted commas, tend to interrupt the flow of the sentence so you should only use them when absolutely necessary. They are useful for technical explanations, acknowledgements of sources, or when you want to spell something out in full for the first time and thereafter use initials. These are all examples of brackets used properly:

McPhail argues that business contains so many imponderables that reward can never be reliably linked to results. (*Harvard Business Review*, May 1996)

Bill Morris, General Secretary of the Transport and General Workers' Union (TGWU) . . .

Retail prices are now at their lowest level since 1994 (see chart B on page 27).

Remember: good punctuation is not a matter of rules; it's simply about helping the reader to pause in the right places.

Chapter 4
Looking at the words – layout

Good writing is about more than good use of language. It's about presenting your words in an attractive and eye-catching manner. The most beautiful piece of writing will not work if it looks dense or hard to read. Which would you rather read – a solid page of black type with narrow margins, or a page with headings, sub-heads, an easy-to-read typeface and plenty of white space?

Not so long ago, writers were dependent on typesetters and printers for the appearance of their work. Now, with the advent of sophisticated word-processing packages and desk-top publishing, it pays not only to get the words right but also to get involved in presentation and layout.

Before sending any written message, consider the following:

- Don't just read the words; look at the whole page.
- Check that you have appropriate headings to catch the eye.
- Think about white space, and all-round readability.

Creating a good layout

Unlike grammar, there are no recognised standards for good layout and presentation; much of it is to do with personal taste. A good starting point is to look at documents that you have in the office: letters, memos, faxes, reports, forms, adverts. Select the ones you like best in each category. Examine them to find what it is that makes them attractive. Is it:

- The size of the paper?
- The typeface?
- Use of white space?
- Columns?
- Illustrations?
- The way the text is organised?

Make a list of the features that appeal to you. Then choose the literature you like least, and list the things that irritate you. By the end of this exercise you will have some idea what you are looking for – and what you don't want. Even if you don't create the actual layout and presentation yourself, you will be able to tell the professionals how you would like your work to look.

Three key ingredients

There are three key ingredients in basic text layout: column width, leading (pronounced 'ledding', and meaning the space allowed between lines), and type style.

Column width

The general rule is that single columns should have between 8 and 12 words per line. Which of these is easier to read?

EXAMPLE 1

Penguin Books built much of its success on understanding that the human eye can only absorb a limited amount of text across the page. They introduced broad margins and narrow columns to attract the reader to their paperbacks. The same applies to business writing.

EXAMPLE 2

Penguin Books built much of its success on understanding that the human eye can only absorb a limited amount of text across the page. They introduced broad margins and narrow column widths to attract the reader to their paperbacks. The same applies to business writing.

Don't feel you have to put as much as possible onto one page. You want to create a good impression, so give the reader time to absorb your words and to look forward to what is coming next. Don't clutter up the page with words; use wide margins and don't worry if your text stops halfway down a page. Word processors allow you to set the margins top and bottom, and left and right. Experiment with different margin sizes until you think it looks good.

Leading

Leave plenty of space between paragraphs, but don't let them look isolated or disconnected. If you use headings between paragraphs, leave at least as much space above the text as below.

EXAMPLE 1

HEADING

Leave plenty of space between paragraphs, but don't let them look isolated or disconnected. If you use headings between paragraphs, leave at least as much space above the text as below.

EXAMPLE 2

HEADING

Leave plenty of space between paragraphs, but don't let them look isolated or disconnected. If you use headings between paragraphs, leave at least as much space above the text as below.

Decide how much space you want between the lines of text, so that the next line is single-spaced, 1.5 line-spaced or double-spaced. Most text is set with single spacing, but it depends on the context. With a first draft of a report, for instance, you will want to leave space for comments. The wider the column, the more space you need between lines.

Type style

Choose which type size you want. Type is measured in 'point' sizes and, in most typefaces, 9-point and above is legible for large areas of text. Most books are printed in 9-point; most letters are 11- or 12-point. Remember, though, that the typeface – the 'font' – will affect how big the type looks:

This is 11-point 'Book Antiqua', a classic font available on most PCs

This is 11-point 'Bookman Old Style' – it appears larger than the previous one, although it is the same point size.

Try out different fonts. One good way of doing this is to print out all the fonts on your PC so you know all the options available. Most word-processing packages carry more than 30 styles.

Different fonts suit different circumstances. If you were producing a huge glossy advertisement you would go for big, dramatic lettering. But in general, type for body text – the main text of booklets, letters and reports – should be unassuming and easy on the eye.

If the text covers a fairly large area, most people prefer a serif face, such as 'Times New Roman' or the Bookman Old Style font shown above, the design for which has little legs or serifs coming out from the vertical strokes. Serifs guide the eye horizontally, which is why most newspapers and publishers use fonts designed with them. Although serif faces come in many shapes and forms, they all look classical and important.

Sans-serif (without serifs) typefaces come into their own as headings and in forms, leaflets, advertisements and any situation where a bright, clear typeface is needed. They can be used for large blocks of text, but they are less easily read. In the end, it's largely a matter of personal preference. On the whole, books look better in serif typefaces, while business letters, press releases and brochures often look better in sans-serif faces. Examples of sans-serif faces include 'Arial', 'Century Gothic', 'Gill', 'Helvetica' and 'Univers'.

Another consideration is whether or not to 'justify' the text, by getting all the lines of type to line up on the left or right (or both). Again, it's a matter of preference. Justification is more formal and gives documents a disciplined look. Unjustified type is more informal, with lines ending at different places on the page. Again, experiment on your PC.

Enhancements

Many people use CAPITAL LETTERS to emphasise a point they want highlighted in a document but, in practice, words in lower case are easier to read:

THIS IS HARD TO READ BECAUSE
ALL THE WORDS HAVE THE SAME SHAPE

This is easier to read
because the words look different

Use bold to emphasise. *Italics can be used, but they are more difficult to read*, and are most often used in quotations, titles of works or foreign phrases. <u>Underlining can be used for headings, or to stress words or phrases, but can easily make the page look cluttered.</u>

➡ VARYING LAYOUT WITH THE TYPE OF DOCUMENT

Now let's look at different types of written material. The style and layout will vary depending on the sort of communication being produced.

Letters

Most businesses use A4-sized paper printed with the company logo and details. Look carefully at the typeface used for the letterhead, and where on the page the logo falls. Is the design across the top of the page or down one of the sides? Is the typeface spiky or round? Is it elegant and sophisticated or big and brash? The typeface you choose for your letter will depend on the typeface used in the letterhead.

If your company's logo is bright and cheerful and uses a sans-serif typeface, it is wrong to write a letter in an elegant, formal serif type because it will clash. You might not want to choose anything as demanding as the logo typeface, but you will want a style that complements it. Similarly, if your letterhead is neat and unassuming, a big sans-serif face will look completely out of place.

Now for the design. If your logo is spread across the top of the page, you will probably want to put your text in one column down the middle of the page. If the logo is down the right- or left-hand side, it's better to reduce the width of your column to give the logo space. By and large, letters are not justified to both margins, and if it's a short letter, justification on the right looks silly. However, if it's a long, formal letter it will probably look better justified at left and right (like this book).

Try laying out the text on the page as neatly as possible. Put the address in the top left-hand corner. Commas after each line are not necessary; in fact, it looks better without commas. Keep the paragraphs and the spacing neat.

Memos

Many businesses have standard memo forms. If you want to design one for yourself, use plain paper. Make it clear who is sending the memo, to whom it is addressed, and what the subject is. The main thing is to make it look businesslike. A standard memo could look like that shown in figure 4.1.

MEMO

To: From:

Ref: Date:

Message:

Figure 4.1: A sample memo form

Faxes

As with memo pads, many companies have standard fax forms. When faxes were first possible to produce and send, people tended to print 'Fax Fax Fax' across the top. As they are so common nowadays and as the distinguishing features of sending number/time are shown, there is no need to do this. Nevertheless, it is still helpful if the word 'fax' appears somewhere at the top of the first page, so that it is not confused with a photocopied letter.

Make sure that the name of the person receiving the fax is very obvious – lots of faxes go to one central machine in an office, and you want to make sure that the right person gets it as quickly as possible. You also need to make sure that the number of pages is included.

Figure 4.2 shows one way of formatting a fax heading, but there are plenty of others.

---

fax
_____

To: Rosemary Greensleeves
                     Accounts Department

No. pages   12
(inc. this cover)

From: Miss Scarlett
                     Hi-Top Printers

Ref: Your Annual Report

Date: 19 December 1999

If you have any problems reading this fax, or some of the pages have not come through, please phone xxxxxxx

---

Figure 4.2: A sample fax heading sheet

Reports

Reports, particularly annual reports, are often produced by professional designers. But plenty of internal reports are simply generated by individuals and produced on their own PCs. Here are a few guidelines to remember.

If you are sending a report (or even a letter) that includes a lot of figures, a table is a more effective way of giving the information than words. Imagine that you need to tell a client about the value of their pension. You could write:

You have three pension plans with XXX company. The first pension is due to mature in six months' time and will be worth £12,000 per year. The second one will mature in 2006 and is currently valued at £5,000 per year. The third plan will mature in 2010 and is valued at today's prices at £25,000 per year.

Or you could create a table, as shown in Table 4.1, which is a very straightforward process on a PC. Not only does this avoid unnecessary words; it also makes it much easier to absorb the information at a glance.

Your three pension plans

Year you took out the plan	1979	1986	1980
Current value per annum	£12,000	£5,000	£25,000
Date of maturity	1999	2006	2010

Table 4.1

There are many other examples of information that can be displayed more easily using a table. Here is a letter from a local organisation about the cost of hiring a room for a meeting:

The Green Hall is available for parties of up to 40 people. The basic cost is £7.50 per hour, but if you need tables and chairs, it costs extra. We charge 50p for every chair, plus an additional £2.50 for every hour you stay after 9 p.m.

LOOKING AT THE WORDS – LAYOUT

The writer could have used a table instead, as shown in Table 4.2.

Hire Rates for the Green Hall	
Hire of room 7–9 p.m.	*£7.50*
Hire of room after 9 p.m.	*£2.50 per hour*
Hire of chairs	*£0.50 per chair*

Table 4.2

The table makes it much easier to work out the overall cost – and ensure that the meeting is over by 9 p.m!

Using graphs is another way of getting information across easily, and most word-processing packages contain a simple graphics system to help you do this. For example, a company wanting to explain the geographic spread of its employees could write:

> *As of June 1998, Bluebottle Matches has 1000 employees, of whom 10% are in the Midlands, 10% are in Scotland, 30% are in Wales, and the rest are in the South-East.*

A graphical representation, such as that in Figure 4.3, is much easier to take in at a glance.

```
Bluebottle Matches: geographical spread of employees (June 1998)

                        MIDLANDS: 100
                                  SCOTLAND: 100
    SOUTH EAST: 500

                                  WALES: 300

TOTAL: 1000 employees
```

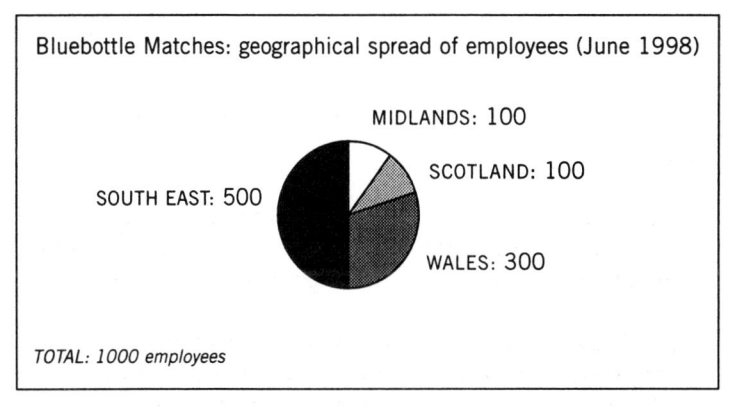

Figure 4.3: A sample pie chart

Instructions and manuals

The same rules apply to writing manuals as to reports. Whether it's a simple manual explaining how to fix a hose-pipe onto a tap, or a complicated one describing how to assemble and connect up a complex piece of machinery, the instructions must be clear.

Use simple headings, straightforward language and as many illustrations as possible. The following example of how to assemble a desk would tax the brains of Einstein:

> *Assemble the single parts, nos 1–7 (see picture). Align them in order 1, 4 and 7. Screw them into pieces 2, 3, 5 and 6. Insert the screws using the special screwdriver (included). Turn the desk over. Insert the stoppers in the prepared holes in the base. If the stoppers are provided with filletted pins, screw them in. Once each stopper is screwed in, turn the desk over. Place the top of the desk (8) onto pieces 2, 3, 5 and 6. Attach these to the base, insert the screws and cover with the holding stops.*

This masterpiece of explanation was accompanied by three illustrations: the single parts; the screws and the filletted pins (but not the special screwdriver); and the finished product. It took five hours to assemble, and even then there was a piece left over. A stage-by-stage diagram, with clear instructions that related to each action, would have been much simpler and less traumatic to follow.

The same rules apply to any instruction manual. Be simple, be clear and use as many illustrations as possible. In such instances, pictures tell you far more than any number of words.

➡ SUMMARY

Now that most people have access to modern technology, it's much easier to produce good-looking documents that will attract the reader's attention. It may mean that you have to spend a bit of

LOOKING AT THE WORDS – LAYOUT

time learning how to use the various programmes on your PC, but it's worth it. You can be flexible, you can use your imagination, and you can then produce strong, effective documents that look good and complement your words.

So please:

- use your technology
- make life easier for the reader
- keep the layout clear
- and make sure it complements your words.

Part 2
Writing for results

In Part 1, we looked at the tools a business writer needs. In the next six chapters we look at how to apply those tools to various tasks. Above all, we will be writing for results, either in terms of conveying messages, selling things, or encouraging our readers to respond in particular ways.

Chapter 5
What's the form?

There are a few vital principles to remember, whatever you are writing. Even the simplest memo must be properly constructed if you want to make your point clearly. If it's a short message, you can probably keep the outline in your head. If it's a longer letter or some kind of report or whatever, it usually helps to write down the main points then put them in the order in which you think they will be most effective.

Before you launch into print, consider the following:

1. Do I need to write, and if so, why? People often write things down when they could just as easily deal with them by a phone call or a private word.

2. Once you've decided that you do need to write, think about who is going to read it. What sort of document is appropriate? What will the readership expect? What will be most helpful for them? And what will be most helpful for you?

3. Now you have identified your likely readers and decided on the appropriate form, you need to think about tone. How familiar should you be? What is most likely to prompt the desired reaction?

   If you can avoid it, don't use a standard format that will read as if the document has come off a production line (see examples in the next section). Whether it's a simple memo or a long report, put yourself in the place of the reader: What would I want this document to say? How would I want it to sound?

   The answers are bound to vary according to the type of document, but in general you want the tone to reflect the content. For example, a letter offering a job should be friendly, but clear and factual. A letter of complaint might require slightly more distance between writer and reader. An apology must be sincere; a report informative and interesting; and a request polite but persuasive. Whatever the scenario, each message should have its own distinct voice, and should leave the reader or readers feeling that *they* are important.

4. Once you've decided on purpose, form and tone, think about content. What do I need to say? What does the reader need to know? What else might they like to know? What will persuade them to react in the way I want?

    Scribble down some ideas, then try to narrow them down. Remember Pascal and the short letter he wanted to write. The shorter you can make it, the more effective the message is likely to be. Many business writers cram far too much information into a document because, subconsciously, they worry that they are not getting their point across – and they end up boring their readers.

Once you have the answers to the questions, it's time to start writing. But how should you start? In this chapter, we're primarily concerned with form – beginnings and endings. In the next chapter, we will look in greater depth at content.

➡ OPENING MOVES

The first thing the reader of a letter, memo or fax will see is their name, address and the date. It's very important to get these right, and yet it is remarkable how often people misspell names, or give incorrect titles. If you are in any doubt, call first to check spelling and other details. Then lay them out neatly on the page.

Start with the address in the top left-hand corner. Commas after each line of the address are unnecessary, and look untidy. Putting 'Esq' after a man's name has gone out of fashion, but if you think an older reader would appreciate it, then use it. For the address on the envelope and at the top of the letter, it is normally sufficient simply to give the person's name, without Mr, Miss, Mrs or Ms. But when it comes to the 'Dear...' men and women should be addressed as Mr or Ms unless you know their title (e.g. Chief Superintendent), or you know that the female reader in question would prefer to be 'Miss' or 'Mrs'. If that's the case, use their chosen title – few things annoy some people more than being labelled 'Ms' if they've made it clear they are 'Miss' or 'Mrs'.

It can get complicated knowing how to address titled people. In general, use their title and surname unless you know them well: 'Dear Chief Superintendent Davidson' (for example) is the safest form of address and cannot offend. For knights or baronets, (as an instance) 'Sir David Munroe' in the address, but 'Dear Sir David' in the letter. Peers of the realm are normally addressed by their full title on the envelope, then as 'Dear Lord (or Lady) Whatever'. If you're writing to a peer, a bishop or a member of the Royal Family, it is best to consult a book on etiquette or ring the person's office to check the form. Earl Russell, a hereditary peer, recently received a letter addressed to 'Earl Russell Lords', which began 'Dear Mr Earl Lords' instead of 'Dear Lord Russell'.

Writing to people you don't know is also difficult. Few people like being addressed as 'Dear Sir/Madam'. It's impersonal and can seem insulting as the writer has obviously not bothered to find out the recipient's sex, let alone their name. In these days of mailing lists and electronic databases, there is usually no excuse for leaving out someone's name.

There are times, however, when you want to write a large number of direct-mail letters. In such instances, you can address the reader as 'Dear Customer', 'Dear Supporter' or even 'Dear Friend', but only use the latter if you or your organisation know the client group well; it can easily seem presumptuous.

References can either go under the address or on the opposite side of the page. Make the date clear as well. And don't just type in numerals – it looks lazy. Write the month and year in full. Both 16th October 1992 and 16 October 1992 are acceptable in the UK (some other countries tend to reverse the day and month), if you are using the 'th', make sure you use it throughout the document.

The following is a standard address to a reader:

Jane Brown
43 The Willows
Dendridge
HT98 0PP   Our ref:

6 July 1999

Dear Ms Brown

(No comma is required after 'Dear Ms Brown', although it is a matter of taste.)

Once you have said 'hello', let the reader know what the letter is about. Most business letters benefit from a heading as it introduces the topic and saves having to write a complicated first sentence. Headings, usually underlined or in bold type – again a matter of preference – should state the subject clearly. It doesn't matter if they run to several lines.

Dear Ms Brown

Green Trees Critical Illness Cover:
Policy No 60606060, Renewal Date

It used to be traditional to start the headings with 're' or 'ref', but there is no need for these abbreviations nowadays as they merely clutter the page.

Now let's look at some openings:

EXAMPLE 1

Jane Brown
43 The Willows
Dendridge
HT98 0PP   *Our ref: 6–427931*

6 May 1999

Dear Ms Brown

Ref: Green Trees Critical Illness Cover:
Policy No 60606060 Renewal Date 23rd June 1999

With reference to the above policy, we are writing to inform you that your policy falls due for renewal on 23rd June. Should you wish to make any amendments to the policy, the enclosed forms must be returned, completed, by that date.

EXAMPLE 2

Jane Brown
43 The Willows
Dendridge
HT98 0PP   Our ref: 6-427931

6 May 1999

Dear Ms Brown

Green Trees Critical Illness Cover
Policy No 60606060, Renewal Date 23 June 1999

Your Critical Illness Cover is due for renewal by 23 June. If you wish to make any changes to the policy, please complete and return the enclosed forms.

At first glance, Example 1, may seem a reasonable letter – until you compare it with Example 2. The first one then comes across as pompous and unnecessarily long-winded. There is no need to say 'with reference to . . .', as the reference is given immediately above. And there is no need to say 'we are writing' as that's self-evident. The first 13 words of the first version can simply be deleted. The letter sounds so much more professional without the padding.

Your job at the beginning of any written communication is to give the reader the context. Avoid phrases like 'With reference to your letter of the 25th instant . . .' or 'Further to your letter of . . .'. Remember what we said earlier about being conversational? Why use these starchy phrases that have no place in everyday language? 'Thank you for your letter dated 25 May' is all you need. Don't be afraid to start with a short sentence, but make sure it is complete: 'Regarding your claim for housing benefit.' is not a sentence; 'Your claim for housing benefit has been referred to me.' is much better. If in doubt, simply tell the story so far. 'You wrote to us on 23

October to enquire about fixed-rate mortgages.' 'Since our telephone conversation of 12 April, I have investigated your complaint.' 'Your advertisement on page 4 of today's *Guardian* caught my eye.'

We have been discussing letters, but the same guidance applies to memos, faxes and e-mail messages. Give the reader the context, and get to the point as quickly as possible.

➡ SIGNING OFF

Before you sign off any document, check that you have left a clear impression. This is your last chance to remind the reader of the main point of your message – or, in some cases, of the action they should take. So don't waste it.

> Please send your cheque no later than 18 June 2000.
>
> I look forward to receiving your application shortly.

Or maybe you just want to sign off in a friendly way, showing that you care:

> Have a great holiday!

Please don't conclude with the dreadfully overused 'If you have any further queries, please do not hesitate to call.' This is formulaic, non-conversational language, used only in business letters. If you've done your job properly, why should there be any queries? Anyway, if the reader does have any queries, will they not have the wit to call the number given at the top of your letter?

So how do you sign off? Unless you know the person by their first name, 'Yours sincerely' is the usual form. 'Yours faithfully' can be saved for those letters that began 'Dear Sir/Madam' or 'Dear Customer' or 'Dear Supporter'. More informal endings such as 'Regards' or 'Kind regards' are at your discretion, but be wary of using them in letters to strangers or people you hardly know. Not everybody likes them. 'Best wishes' is probably the safest of those informal endings.

Marketing people love to add a PS (Postscript) after signing – for the simple reason that these brief messages stand out, and almost always get read. But a PS looks sloppy in a formal business letter. Save them for sales letters.

➡ SUMMARY

- Address the right person, by name.
- Get to the point.
- Be approachable, but not overfamiliar.
- Leave a clear impression.

Chapter 6
Writing that Works

Having looked at beginnings and endings, we must now address the content of letters. The rest of this chapter examines various different types of letters (and applies equally to faxes and memos) and gives examples of how – and how not – to write.

The subjects are:

- Applications and requests
- Complaint and apology
- Introductions and references
- Dismissal, rejection and resignation
- Explanation and clarification

➡ APPLICATIONS AND REQUESTS

This section looks at applications and requests – for services, favours, payment etc. – for which many of the same principles apply. The common factor is that they are all personal. You are applying for something that matters to you, and you need to find the right balance between forcefulness and politeness, assertiveness and modesty.

Applications

Job applications and letters of invitation contain elements of salesmanship, and are dealt with in the next chapter. An application for a pension or a bank loan should be easier, so long as you have all the information at your fingertips and can explain the situation in a straightforward way. No bank manager will offer a loan to someone who writes a long letter about their personal circumstances without a single mention of their financial expectations. Work out exactly how much money you want and how you can pay for it. If you're not clear about the information the reader will need, don't worry about looking ignorant – write and ask for it:

Henry Boyle
Midshire Bank plc
Upper Park Road
London

11 June 1997

Dear Mr Boyle

Account Nos 1234567 and 2345678

I need to increase my overdraft on the above accounts, but am unsure about the information you need to authorise the loan. Please would you let me know what you want? Thank you.

Applying to join a membership organisation or a trade association is much the same. If you wish to join, for example, a private club that has a waiting list, explain clearly why you are so enthusiastic. You might want to become a member of Paragliders International because you like the idea of going out with your mates to lovely countryside – but can you paraglide? Ask a member to endorse your application and give you a good reference:

Paragliders International
Top Hole Hill
Wychwood Vale
Gloucestershire
GL3 1YW

27 May 1998

Dear Paragliders International

I enclose my application form for membership of your organisation along with a reference from a current member. I took up paragliding three years ago and am an enthusiastic member of Flying High. I now want to become a member of Paragliders International, as I feel I am ready to compete in international competitions and would appreciate the help and support you provide.

Yours sincerely

A trade association will have criteria that you or your organisation must meet. Find out what these are before you apply. If you don't meet the conditions, you won't get in.

The key to making successful applications is research. Find out exactly what the employer/bank/organisation wants before you start writing. Work out what you have to offer – whether it's money, commitment or expertise – and outline your qualifications clearly. If necessary, seek out good references.

Like applications, requests should be carefully researched. Even if you're simply asking an organisation to send you a brochure be sure to specify which brochure, which area of operation, which dates etc. Writing to the English National Opera just asking for a catalogue could mean anything, and the chances are you won't get anything as it's not worth their while to write back; if you write and ask for a brochure for the autumn/winter season 1999, you will get exactly what you want.

Requests

Requests are often for several items from one supplier. Use lists to make it easy for the sender – it'll speed up your order and should guarantee good service. Compare the following letters:

EXAMPLE 1

Bluegrass Perfumes Ltd
Onyx Industrial Centre
Hambledon
SX2 4JZ

7 July 1998

Dear Bluegrass Perfumes,

I would like to purchase some of your products, and hope you can send me three bottles of Bluenight eau-de-cologne, five jars of night repair unguent and eight boxes of bluegrass eau-de-toilette wipes. I think this comes to £140 and enclose a cheque for that amount.

Yours faithfully,

EXAMPLE 2

Bluegrass Perfumes Ltd
Onyx Industrial Centre
Hambledon
SX2 4JZ

7 July 1998

Dear Bluegrass Perfumes,

Please would you send me the following products:

3 bottles Bluenight eau-de-cologne @ £14.50 each	£43.50
5 jars night repair unguent @ £9.50 each	£47.50
8 boxes Bluegrass eau-de-toilette wipes @ £6.50 each	£52.00
	£143.00

I enclose a cheque for the full amount.

Yours faithfully,

The first letter contains all the information, but is not clear and does not include the individual prices. As a result, the author cannot count the total cost, and has sent a cheque for the wrong amount. The second letter is much clearer; the list is easily read; and the total is calculated (correctly).

Other types of request include demands for payment or services. Make invoices simple and itemise each purchase so that the buyer knows exactly what they are being charged for. Include VAT separately (where chargeable).

If you're asking for a service, put the subject of the letter up front, and explain clearly what you need. Say, for example, that you have commissioned someone to build new cupboards in your office. Don't just assume that a verbal agreement will mean that the work is done to schedule and on time; write the supplier a letter stating exactly what you want from them, and when you expect the work to be completed. If there are any penalty clauses, mention them in the letter. If they don't like it, it's up to them to negotiate. At least you've got your brief on paper, which gives you a measure of control and makes you much better placed in the event of any dispute.

If you have to chase someone who hasn't paid a bill, start by being polite but firm, while offering a conditional apology in case your letter has crossed with their payment ('If your payment has crossed with this letter, we're sorry to have bothered you.'). Send the reminder along with a stamped, addressed envelope to encourage payment. If nothing happens for two weeks after that, and enough weeks have elapsed to take account of the fact that someone may have been on holiday (perhaps 2–3 weeks after your stipulated last date for payment), you may well have to get tough. Assuming telephone calls have also been unproductive, you might write something like this:

Dear Miss Ewart,

Second reminder: Invoice No 1276

It is now three weeks since we wrote to you, reminding you of this unpaid invoice, and we have yet to receive a reply. Our terms are clearly stated, and you have never queried them.

I enclose copies of previous correspondence, which has been strictly one-way. We cannot ignore this debt any longer, and if we do not hear from you within 10 days of the date on this letter, the matter will be placed in the hands of our solicitors.

Yours sincerely,

Other requests for money may require subtlety rather than firmness. With a fund-raising appeal, for instance, it is usually unwise to make a full frontal assault on the reader's conscience. There comes a point for the reader when sympathy gives way to the realisation that nothing you can do is going to make very much difference. The cynical phrase is 'compassion fatigue'. To counteract this, many charities opt for the more personal approach – 'Adopt an orphan', 'Adopt a granny' or 'Adopt a wild animal' – so that readers can receive updates on the progress of a single living being, and can feel that their contribution is making a real difference.

You can do the same by making it clear, for instance, that every £10 towards the community hall roof appeal buys a single slate or tile, or every £20 for the literacy appeal buys eight paperback classics or four computer mice. People can be quite generous if they think they are making a difference.

When making a request or application:

- Find out everything you can about your readers, and what they want.
- Address all the essential criteria, or explain the salient facts.
- Use every connection – references, recommendations, inducements – to make the request personal.

➡ COMPLAINTS AND APOLOGIES

Letters of complaint and apology can be equally difficult. Many complainants spoil their case by overstating it; many respondents forget that surrender is often easier and more effective than self-defence.

Complaints

Let's start with complaint. The commonest mistake is to write in anger, to vent your frustration. Write such complaints by all means, but then tear them up. If you want results, calm down and think about what you might achieve by a measured complaint, supported by incontrovertible evidence.

Contrast these two faxes of complaint:

EXAMPLE 1

Bill Smith
Plumbers and Carpenters
Green Lane
Bloggsville
BG1 4LL

Fax No: 01654–321321

Dear Mr Smith,

I've just got back to the office to find that our reception is three feet deep in water, ducks have moved into my office, and the water has turned green. What do you think you were doing? All I wanted you to do was replace the old boiler, not turn the office into a swimming pool. If you don't get over here and fix it as soon as you get this letter, I'm going to the police.

Robert Sykes

Entertaining but intemperate! The reader will think the biggest problem he has to deal with is the client, not the boiler. This sort of letter does not encourage suppliers to remedy mistakes quickly or take trouble over their work.

EXAMPLE 2

Bill Smith
Plumbers and Carpenters
Green Lane
Bloggsville
BG1 4LL

Fax No: 01654–321321

Dear Mr Smith,

Boiler replacement at Sykes and Green

I have just returned to my office to find that the boiler you were contracted to mend has started leaking badly. We have spoken about the problem on the phone, but I also want to put my concern in writing in case the matter has to go further. It may be that the problem is not your fault, but whatever the situation, I expect you to mend the boiler immediately. I will withhold your fee until the work is completed satisfactorily.

Robert Sykes

Angry, but controlled and temperate. The supplier, who probably had no personal responsibility for the mistake, is offered the chance to put things right. And the threat of withholding money adds a powerful sense of urgency.

The second fax above obeys all the cardinal rules of a written complaint, which are to:

- state the facts as objectively as possible
- give the reader a chance to put things right
- threaten serious consequences if nothing is done
- keep the language restrained.

Apologies

A measured complaint such as this should, with luck, elicit a response like this, which contains a suitable apology:

Robert Sykes
Sykes and Green
Duck Pond Lane
Bloggsville
BG2 4RS

Dear Mr Sykes,

I am extremely sorry to hear about the problems you have been having with your boiler. I have instructed workmen to visit your office immediately, and while I cannot take full responsibility until I know all the details, I will be taking a personal interest in the situation.

This letter recognises the client's problem, shows willingness to respond immediately, and should help to keep tempers under control. At the same time, it reserves the right to apportion blame where it truly belongs – wherever that turns out to be. It is not unconditional surrender.

Now here's an example of how not to respond to a complaint:

Dear Mr Jones,

Thank you for your letter dated 13/7/97 explaining both your satisfaction as well as your frustration which is fully understandable to appreciate. All comments made by yourself are not entirely true regarding information passed but are accepted in total as constructional criticism in the hopes that a repeat situation such as endured by you does not ensue. Would you please accept our sincere apologies from all within our company as we do not wish to leave anybody with a sour taste and find enclosed the typed guarantee. Once again please accept our profuse apologies for an unacceptable delay which became beyond our control as it stemmed from the extruding suppliers.
© Plain English Campaign

The English is so convoluted that it ends up being almost endearing. It would have been much better if it had read:

Dear Mr Jones

Thank you for your letter of 13 July 1997 and your compliments. We are sorry that you have had problems and appreciate your concern. Although we have not yet discovered which, if any, of our employees gave you incorrect information, we accept your criticisms.

Please accept our apologies and our typed guarantee.

The big mistake is to go immediately on the defensive. As an increasing number of businesspeople are becoming aware, a complaint requiring an apology can offer a real opportunity to win a customer's loyalty. If you pursue the complaint with sufficient vigour, you may be able to provide the customer with a level of personal service that will encourage them to do business with you for a good while.

Above all, try to see things from the reader's point of view. For example, if you had written to a company complaining about a product, you would want an immediate answer, an apology and, probably, some compensation. The first thing the company must do is acknowledge the letter and the complaint, however trivial or invalid they may consider it to be. There is nothing worse from the customer's point of view than receiving a letter that misses the point or that implies that the complainant is at fault.

Even if the customer is wrong in certain respects, give them the benefit of the doubt, be polite and don't enter into a debate about detail. The same applies to a disagreement with a colleague or partner firm. Be reasonable and see what you can do to improve the situation. You should not make apologies too effusive; that can give the impression of inefficiency. If you apologise, simply say sorry; don't make excuses or try to shift the blame. The customer just wants an apology and some acceptance of fault on your part.

These are the essential elements of a written apology:

- address the customer's concerns directly
- apologise if necessary, but don't grovel
- explain what you are doing to put things right
- avoid arguing about details.

➡ INTRODUCTIONS AND REFERENCES

Letters of introduction

Letters of introduction can range from a friendly note to someone you know, to a formal business letter. Even if the subject of the letter is not well known to you, make sure the name of the person, business or product is one of the first things the reader sees. If it's a note to an acquaintance, start with the context and then move on to the introduction. For example:

> Dear James,
>
> When we met last week you said you were looking for a volunteer to help out in the office. I've thought of someone who might be very good. Her name is Susan Blythe, she's just finished a degree in business administration and she is interested in your type of work. I've

known her for ten years, and she's always been helpful and intelligent. If it's all right with you, I'll ask her to contact you.

Another approach is to introduce yourself or your business. This needs to be more formal and must get to the point at once:

Peter Green
Economic Development Manager
Littleton County Council
Town Hall
Daisy Lane
Littleton
LT4 1JU

10 June 1998

Dear Mr Green,

Single Regeneration Budget (SRB) Financial Systems

As a successful SRB applicant, you will have to develop financial management systems that are acceptable to the Department of Environment, Transport and the Regions. My firm, Data and Delivery, has been developing SRB financial systems for local authorities for over five years and is widely recognised as an expert in the field. We can offer you a purpose-designed system compatible with your other systems, which will meet all the Government's criteria and save you hours of work.

I enclose a brochure outlining our services. I am happy to discuss your requirements without charge.

Yours sincerely,

Walter Evans
Sales Manager

This letter alerts the local authority to an impending management task, at the same time introducing the company. It offers free advice without committing the reader to doing anything. The writer gets straight to the point, mentions the important subject, and doesn't introduce irrelevant information.

Introductory letters may sometimes need to be formal, but

they don't need to be stilted. A letter that begins 'This is to introduce Susan Blythe' loses the personal touch. If you know the person you are writing to, keep it chatty, informal – and short. Letters of introduction are just that; their role is to encourage the reader to take further action, not to make an open-and-shut case.

Faxes and other electronic communications can also be useful media for introductions, although you must be sure to label your message so as to mark it out from the deluge of junk mail that arrives by fax (or 'spam', as it is known on e-mail).

For notes of introduction, three tips:

- Mention the name in the first paragraph.
- Keep it personal.
- Keep it short.

References

References are subtly different from introductions. A reference not only introduces the person or product but it also reflects on you. Your credibility is tied up in what you say about the person or object, so it's important to be quite sure that you want to be associated with the subject of the letter. Don't just dash off a reference because you feel sorry for someone; it won't do them or you any favours.

Be sure that you mean what you say. It is possible to write references that damn with faint praise, and there are times when this is unavoidable, but they are very difficult to do well and usually leave a nasty taste in your mouth. Try to avoid them.

There are two sorts of reference:

- specific ones requested by a potential employer or purchaser
- more general ones, which accompany speculative letters.

The first type is not as easy to write as it seems at first glance. Prospective employers or purchasers often ask for details that relate to the job or activity. Read carefully the letter that is asking for a reference and make a note of the points on which the author wants clarification. It's no use writing a glowing reference about what an excellent bookkeeper someone is when they are applying for a job as an economist.

The following example is a response to a request about someone applying to be director of a charity. The referee was asked to comment on the applicant's management and fund-raising skills, and their ability to deal with delicate situations.

Hilary Payne
Crime Prevention Trust
London
NW21 4JA

3 January 1997

Dear Ms Payne,

Stewart Lock

Thank you for your letter dated 22 December 1996 asking for a reference for Stewart Lock. I'm pleased to be able to recommend him without hesitation. I've known him for five years, since he became Director of The Open Windows Trust. In his time here, he has turned the organisation round.

When he started at Open Windows, the charity had an annual turnover of £65,000. We now have a turnover of some £2 million per annum, largely thanks to Stewart's fund-raising skills and his ability to network with the charitable sector, business and statutory agencies. Much of our work involves difficult negotiations with professionals from various disciplines, but Stewart mastered the intricacies very quickly, and developed strong relationships.

He has strong management skills, although he is also good at letting people work independently if it suits them. He is inclined to be impetuous, but that's a positive benefit in a competitive and difficult area like ours. He is a good communicator and an imaginative lateral thinker.

I am confident Stewart will be an effective Director of the Crime Prevention Trust, and I look forward to hearing about his progress.

Yours sincerely,

Jean Bowers

Chair, Open Windows

This reference addresses both the specific questions in the letter from the Crime Prevention Trust and more general skills. The writer also adds a personal touch – looking forward to hearing about the subject's progress – which adds to the effectiveness of her letter.

The other sort of reference is a more general one, often used by people writing to an organisation asking if there is, or might be, a vacancy. It is usually sent with a CV and covering letter, and runs along the lines of:

> To whom it may concern.
>
> I have known Alison Clark for ten years, both as an employee and subsequently as a friend. She has worked in telesales since 1990, and is very good at talking to people on the phone. She has a quick grasp of subjects and goes out of her way to be helpful. She is now looking for work as a manager in a telesales department, a job for which she is well qualified. I am delighted to recommend her.

The principal rules of reference writing are:

- be sure that you want to write the reference
- be honest
- answer *all* the potential employer's questions
- add a personal note.

➡ DISMISSALS REJECTIONS AND RESIGNATIONS

Dismissal

Warning or dismissal letters must follow the guidelines in your company's disciplinary procedure, not least because of the possibility that a warning will lead to a dismissal.

Warning letters must be clear and cover all the issues, for they may be used in subsequent legal actions. Under current employment legislation, employees must have two written warnings before they can be sacked. The first is usually a reminder of a previous conversation, the second a sterner warning, and the final letter dismisses the employee. At each stage in the process, the employee should be given the chance to explain or solve the problem.

Here are three examples, demonstrating the three-stage process just mentioned:

Helen Smart
TCP Caterers
The Green
Blomsgrove
BG7 4JS

3 November 1997

Dear Helen,

First warning – persistent lateness

It is now over three weeks since I had to speak to you about your repeated lateness.

As you know, your hours of work are 9.30 a.m. to 5.30 p.m., with one hour for lunch. You have not been in before 10 a.m. on any morning for the past fortnight, but you haven't been able to give me a sensible explanation. If you have a problem at home, I would like to help. Please feel free to come and talk to me in confidence and we'll try to find a solution. If we can solve your problems and you arrive on time for the next two weeks, I hope we shall soon be able to put this behind us.

Yours sincerely

Peter Porter
Personnel Manager

Two weeks later, the problem remains:

Helen Smart
TCP Caterers
The Green
Blomsgrove
BG7 4JS

17 November 1997

Dear Helen,

Final warning – persistent lateness

I wrote to you on 3 November about your inability to get into work by 9.30 a.m. Despite my offer of help, you still have not given me an explanation for your lateness, and in the last fortnight you have only once been in by 9.30 a.m.

As a result, I have to send you this final warning letter. I am still available if you wish to come and talk about your problems. But if you cannot get in on time on at least seven occasions in the next fortnight, I will have no alternative but to ask you to leave.

Yours sincerely

Peter Porter
Personnel Manager

Helen, unfortunately, did not heed the warnings:

Helen Smart
TCP Caterers
The Green
Blomsgrove
BG7 4JS

1 December 1997

Dear Helen,

Persistent lateness

Despite one verbal and two written warnings, and considerable efforts on my part to find a solution to your problems, you have been late on eight of the last ten working days. As a result, we have no alternative but to dismiss you from TCP Caterers. I am sorry to have to do this as your work was good when you were here but persistent lateness in an employee is unacceptable to our company.

You will leave at the end of this week, and will be paid up to that date.

Yours sincerely

Peter Porter
Personnel Manager

This process, although long and difficult, gives both employer and employee every chance to resolve the situation. Each stage must be put into writing to protect both parties in case the dismissal results in legal proceedings. Thus:

- keep the first warning friendly
- try to be understanding
- explain clearly the reasons for dismissal.

Rejections

Letters of rejection are also difficult to get right. It's very easy to reject something or someone without giving an explanation or encouraging the recipient to try again, and this approach can cause hurt. Many organisations reject unsuccessful job applicants with words that offer no encouragement or explanation. Not only is it demoralising for the applicant to be rejected without explanation; it is also bad for the organisation. Your business needs to attract good people in the future, and you will do yourself no favours by treating job applicants thoughtlessly.

The following letter is a good example of how to let someone down gently:

Don Barker
14 The Grove
Nettleton
Cambs
CB13 1XJ

4 June 1998

Dear Don

Thank you for coming in for interview on Friday. I'm sorry to have to tell you that your application was not successful.

You were an excellent interviewee, but, compared with one of the other candidates, you did not have the breadth of technical experience we require. If you wish to continue looking for similar work, an advanced computer-training course might help – I'm sure you'll find some advertised in your local library.

If you think I might be able to help, please feel free to phone me.

Yours sincerely

Graham Brown
Director

This letter compliments the candidate on his interview, explains why he failed to get the job, and offers advice. It may take a few minutes to write, but it's worth the effort for the positive effect it has on the candidate. He might reapply some day and become a valued employee. At the very least, he will think well of the company.

Whatever the circumstances, a rejection letter should be sympathetic. It is not hard to find something to praise, while pointing out the objective factors (strength of the competition, lack of particular experience or whatever) that resulted in the failure of an application. On the other hand one disgruntled person can do a remarkable amount of damage to a company's reputation.

Remember:

- take time to write rejection letters
- explain your reasons
- find something encouraging to say.

Resignations

Finally in this section, we come to resignations. Reasons for leaving are many – if it's a straightforward case of finding a new job, write a friendly letter to your employer, because you never know when you might need a reference.

If you're resigning from a membership organisation or club, give a brief explanation so that the group knows why you've left. If it's because you aren't happy with their organisation, explain, but don't be aggressive. You're leaving anyway, so you can afford to be magnanimous. If you're resigning because of financial problems, allude to it because a lot of membership organisations and clubs keep membership open to people who have had to leave for good reasons.

Resignations should be

- explanatory
- friendly, unless you've had a major row
- written in a way that keeps the door open for reapplication or a reference.

➡ EXPLANATIONS AND CLARIFICATIONS

Sometimes you have some explaining to do. There may be nothing to apologise for, and you may not want to disagree with your readers. Nonetheless, there is something on which the record needs to be set straight.

If your reader has got the wrong end of the stick, there should be no problem. You simply have to set out the facts as you understand them. Use the word 'misunderstanding', which is neutral, and does not attribute blame to either side; then stick to the facts. If the explanation becomes technical, pause for a moment and think about how you would explain such a matter to a close friend, or a parent; then write that down. The one thing you mustn't do is make it *more* complicated.

Letters of explanation are easy when you have good news to

convey. Bad news is more difficult, and people in business are often tempted to preface their explanations with all sorts of mitigating factors. Wrong. The longer you take to get to the point, the more you irritate your reader. The trick is to get the bad news out of the way first. Thereafter, things can only get better. Here's an example:

Dear Shareholder

Our interim results provide bad news and good news. First, the bad. In the first half of this financial year, our company recorded a trading loss of £46,000. This appears disappointing, particularly compared with a profit for the previous six months of £125,000. But such a comparison is thoroughly misleading, as it takes no account of one exceptional factor.

Just four months ago, the company installed a new software program to handle all accounts and inventory, at a cost of £100,000. Normally, we would have phased this payment over several months, but in this instance we obtained a 25% discount on the understanding that we paid immediately – which we were happily in a position to do.

The installation of the new systems has meant that we need fewer administrative staff. As a result, we have embarked on a staff reduction programme that will eventually reduce our headcount by 20%. Redundancy payments have been a further distorting factor in our half-yearly results.

The upshot of all this is that our company emerges fitter, with more efficient back-office processes, having survived a period of slack demand in the entire industry. Now we are ready for the challenges of the coming year. I fully expect us to return to profit over the next six months, and I look forward to your continuing support.

Yours sincerely,

Not so bad, after all, then. Why should anyone sell their shares when a major cost has just been negotiated and the omens are good? So much better to write this kind of explanatory letter than allow shareholders to stumble across such figures in the financial pages, when they might indeed be tempted to sell.

Chapter 7
Writing that sells

Writing to sell imposes its own disciplines. You know before you start that you have to make an immediate and favourable impression on your potential customer. You need to distinguish what you have to offer from other similar products. And you need to do it as quickly as possible – the average attention span of someone reading a sales message is around 15 seconds. If you haven't stimulated interest in that time, you've failed.

Before you start writing, jot down the answers to a few questions:

- What is my unique selling point (USP)? Can I really claim that my product/job/organisation is completely different from all others? In what way is it different, or better? Can I explain that in just a few words?

- What is my message (the vehicle for getting the USP across)? Of course your message is that your product or service is outstanding, but how are you going to say that in words that will capture a reader's imagination in less than 15 seconds?

- What is my medium? Is a letter the most effective vehicle? Would a flier be punchier? Perhaps a brochure would be better, or possibly an advertisement?

- What can I offer the customer/client/employer? If you're selling yourself, write down why you think you are worth employing. If it's a product, would a free offer make it more attractive? Think about incentives.

- What would make me want to buy this product? Think of

marketing letters and brochures that you've received: which of them persuaded you to join or take out a subscription? Don't be afraid to adapt other people's ideas.

Once you've written down your answers, read them carefully. Put yourself in the reader's shoes. Have you been reasonably objective, or are you so convinced of the wonder of your product that you've simply written dozens of superlatives? If a stranger were to read your notes, would they understand what you are saying? Are you in danger of boring the reader? (Always remember that your potential customer won't know as much about your product or yourself as you do.) Have you really found the right USP, or have you just invented something to sound good? Ask a colleague or friend for an objective view on what you want to say.

Once you think you've got the right message, choose your medium.

➡ SELLING YOUR SERVICES

Imagine you are a self-employed photocopier engineer hoping to drum up trade. What is the best way of attracting attention? There are a number of different ways:

- fliers put through the letter boxes of local businesses
- leaflets with endorsements
- individual letters.

With fliers or leaflets you should not expect a high percentage response. But a witty cartoon of someone wrestling with a photocopier might just ring a few bells with office managers. Then you have to make your pitch. You might try something like this:

PHOTOCOPIER BLUES?

When your photocopier jams, the toner seems to be on perma-black, or the paper feed goes haywire, don't you wish you could get an expert round to fix it within an hour or two? Help is at hand.

My name is Philip Burns, and I've worked with photocopiers for more than

15 years (manufacturers' training/competence certificates from Xerox, Canon and other leading makes). I live and work in the St Albans area, and am always contactable via my mobile phone.

If you have any kind of problem between now and Christmas, let me come and check it out for you – and as an introductory offer, I'll waive my normal £30 call-out fee.

CALL NOW ON 07007 777777 FOR A FREE CHECK-UP

If you are a visiting hairdresser covering a smaller residential area, hand-delivered letters might be more effective:

The Owner
34 Greentree Lane
Greenford
Yorks
YO55 2SP

July 1998

Dear Householder

<u>Hairdresser at your service</u>

Would you like to have your hair cut, washed or permed at home, when it suits you?

Having worked for seven years at Hair Fair in Bradford, I moved to Shipley four months ago. I've only been working part-time here for three weeks, but here is what three of my new clients have said:

> 'This is the best hairdo I've ever had, bar none.' Mrs E. Sykes, Almond Grove.
>
> 'A really professional job, in just 10 minutes.' Mr M. Byrne, Hillside.
>
> 'You're not charging enough!' Julie Thwaite, Mill Lane.

A cut, wash and dry costs just £10. A simple haircut just £5. Perms £20.

Call now on Shipley 299999, and I'll give you more detailed references.

Yours sincerely

Yvonne Routledge

The letter can easily be made more personal if you are writing to someone as a result of a recommendation from a satisfied customer. Start the letter by saying:

Susan Smith has suggested I write to offer you a hairdo – I did her hair last week, and she seemed very pleased with the result.

and the rest can be much the same as the standard letter.

Keep all sales letters short. But whatever the scenario, there are three vital ingredients:

- a clear benefit the reader can instantly identify (a haircut, a fixed photocopier etc.)
- a reason to choose this particular person (qualifications, testimonials)
- a deal-clincher – the reason to act now (a special offer, a personal recommendation etc.).

If you get a positive response from your sales letter and want to follow it up, write a friendly reply thanking the client for making contact and offering them more details. We've chosen a jobbing gardener as an example this time:

Mrs S. Carpenter
34 Greentree Lane
Greenford
Yorks
YO55 2SP

30 July 1998

Dear Mrs Carpenter

Thank you for getting in touch – and I'm sure Gerry Flintoff will be pleased that you followed up his recommendation. As we agreed on the phone, I will come round next Tuesday at 2 p.m. to prune your roses, mow the lawn and tidy up the pond.

I look forward to meeting you then.

Yours sincerely,

Bert Spade

The letter in this example is not strictly necessary, but it places the relationship on a proper footing by confirming what has been agreed. It gives an impression of organisation and reliability. It is certainly more than you would expect from most jobbing gardeners! But successful sales should always involve good follow-up.

➡ ADVERTISING YOUR WARES

Whether you're advertising in a small local newspaper or in a national broadsheet, the rules are the same. You're competing with dozens of others to grab the attention of the reader. Snappy headlines and clear text are essential. Use logos and headlines imaginatively. Underline the words you want to emphasise, highlight them in **bold**, use different fonts (see Chapter 4).

Advertisements with white-on-black text catch the eye immediately. The advert in Figure 7.1 was in a national newspaper in the Appointments section.

> **"I'M WORTH MORE THAN THIS JOB!"**
>
> More people are changing their careers than ever before. If you want a happier, more rewarding life, talk to our experts for an independent assessment. They'll help you find the best way forward.
>
> *Career Analysts*

Figure 7.1: White-on-black classified ad.

Who doesn't think they're worth more than they are paid? This advertisement was surrounded by others all selling the same type of service, but they didn't have such an instant impact.

Copywriting for advertising is a specialist skill we do not propose to explore fully in this book. Most companies that can afford to take out major adverts in the press and on radio and television employ professionals, either in-house or from an agency.

If, however, you want to take a chance and write your own text for an advert, bear in mind the following tips:

- use short words and sentences
- don't use jargon and technical language
- try to amuse or challenge your readers
- mention the advertiser's name somewhere, even if it isn't up front
- make the layout interesting.

An example is given in Figure 7.2

You get up every morning. What do you do?
Clean you teeth? Wash? Boil the kettle?

Why?
Because you can.

Why?
You've got running water haven't you?
Yes. But what's that got to do with it?

Underbarrow Water of course

Suppliers of the cleanest, sweetest water in the county

For further information phone 01555 333666

Figure 7.2: Example advertising copy

Job advertisements are often a source of unintentional humour, and sometimes they are hard to understand. It is crucial to give a clear explanation of the job and sort of candidate you want; if you don't, you'll spend hours sifting through hopelessly inadequate applications – and all that money spent on advertising will have been wasted.

Relate the advert to your job description and person specification. Start by stating what your organisation does, and the salary. Follow it with a clear description of the job and the experience of the ideal candidate – people interested in your field will read on, others won't, so you won't be wasting people's time. Look at the ads placed by professional recruitment agencies or other people in your business area. Your adverts must be clear, informative and comprehensible – unlike the example found in a national newspaper during 1996 that is given in Figure 7.3.

This advert makes almost every mistake in the book. It does say what the salary is, but that's the only thing it has got right. What is/are Sharp Shooters? What is a 'thought provoking laptop presenter'? What are 'qualifications of merit in your leisure pursuits'? And what on earth is the job?

The same principles of clarity and comprehensibility apply to any type of advertising. The photocopier repairer's flier, for instance, could easily be converted into a small advert in his local paper. Major company advertising is usually done through specialist agencies, but smaller businesses may need to advertise their services. Think about what you want from the advert – and keep thinking about the reader. Stimulating headlines, clear information and something special about your product will help to make your advert stand out from others.

Style note: We have shortened the word 'advertisement' to 'advert' – and on one occasion to 'ad' – from time to time, just because it becomes tedious to keep repeating the longer word. But we would always recommend using the full word in the first instance.

> **SHARP SHOOTERS GO EUROLINK**
>
> QUOTA + NEW BUSINESS SALES
>
> *Achievable £100k (base £25k – £35k) + package*
>
> As a premier provider of IT Human Resources from Consultancy to Contract IT Professionals with demand far outstripping supply, an additional select few are required to assist in the growth and development of our Southern Business Centres. Based in the City, Croydon, Brighton or Winchester, you will be instrumental in optimising our business advantage using state of the art marketing including thought provoking laptop client presenters. Are you 27–37 and possess qualifications of merit both in academia and your leisure pursuits? Have you a high drive and a passion for success? Do you believe that meritocracy will take you to the top and is your knowledge of IT solutions and developing new business a proven track record based on excellence? Then forwarding your CV by fax or post will be the first step in joining an elite group destined for on-going success including membership of our Premier Club where quota + over performance will enjoy Antigua in Spring 97.

Figure 7.3: An example of a poorly worded job advert

➡ JOB APPLICATIONS

Job applications are almost an art form. Some people are so good at them that they always get an interview even when they are hopeless for the job. Whether you are writing a letter accompanied by a CV or simply filling in an application form, you need to explain why you want the job, and why you are suitable for it. Your application is all about selling yourself.

One common mistake is to assume that the potential employer

knows what you are like. Always assume total ignorance. Your explanation of why you want the job will be the only indicator of your character, and can make the difference between success and failure. There are some cardinal rules for job applications:

- Find out as much as you can about the organisation before you apply. You want to know what they are looking for.
- Read the job description, person specification and application form with great care and follow the instructions. Personnel officers like their methods to be respected.
- Explain why you are the best person for the job. Employers need to know that you understand the scope of the job and the organisation and that your experience is relevant to them.
- Above all, think of your application as *you*. It needs to reflect your skills, qualities and relevant experience. It's *your* USP, so make sure it's as powerful as possible.

➡ INVITATIONS

Certain kinds of invitation are really sales documents by another name. Whether it's a friendly invitation for a business cocktail party or a formal invitation to a new product launch, you are asking someone to come and support you and your company.

If you are writing to someone you know, make the message as personal as possible. You want the reader to feel more or less indispensable – that the party will not be the same without them. Here is an example:

Gordon Finch
BG Enterprises
Cleveland House
Montagu Road
Bridgport
EX52 4ZX

4 August 1997

Dear Gordon

Launch of a new network system by Ace Computers

How are you? On 2 October we will be celebrating the launch of our new network system, which I am sure will interest BG Enterprises. The event will take place in the Great Hall at Cleveland House, and we are delighted that Hubert Christoffersen, Chairman of our parent company Ace International, is coming over from Denmark for the occasion.

There will be a formal presentation at 5.30 p.m., followed by a reception. I know that our new system has direct relevance to your work, and would like to show you how it works. I look forward to seeing you.

Please would you phone my secretary to confirm that you will be coming?

Best wishes

David Wood
Sales Director

This type of letter is more difficult to refuse than a formal invitation. The combined lure of being asked by a friend, seeing an important new product and meeting the company chairman should ensure that Gordon Finch will come if he can. You can make this kind of letter even more personal by adding that only your best clients have been invited, and that you can promise them an interesting and enjoyable evening (possibly with the offer of dinner afterwards).

Even if you are sending formal invitations, you can easily add a personal letter explaining why that person will be particularly welcome. Now that the mail merge facility is available on most word processors, it is simple to personalise the letter even if you don't know the recipient.

Few people are immune from flattery, which is one of the salesperson's most effective weapons. But it must be wielded subtly. Here is an example addressed to a potential after-dinner speaker:

Peter Moore
Chief Executive
North Bank Traders
Milton House
Green Street
London EC6 4JN

7 November 1998

Dear Mr Moore

I heard your speech at the IPD conference in Eastbourne last month and resolved there and then that I would try to persuade you to come and address the Exeter Round Table. Now the opportunity has arrived.

Your name is top of our list for one simple reason: I don't believe anyone has thought more deeply about the relationship between art and business. Your IPD speech, I felt, explored ideas and issues that few people had hitherto touched upon. We have several enthusiastic art collectors among our members, and an honourable tradition of supporting local artists. I know the members would be fascinated to hear your views on the connection between art and business.

As you may know, the Round Table is not in a position to pay guest speakers. Nonetheless, our annual dinners have attracted some notable guests in recent years, including Sir John Harvey-Jones and Anita Roddick.

We offer a truly excellent dinner – the Royal Oak Hotel being a new entry in this year's *Good Food Guide* – and a double room for you and your wife if you would like to stay the night. If you were to come on a Friday evening, you might consider making a weekend of it, and exploring Exmoor or the beauties of the South Devon coast. We would be honoured if you would both come.

We usually hold our annual dinners towards the end of April, usually

on a Thursday or Friday, so if you are able to accept, please let me
know as soon as possible and we will fix a date. Finally, the timing of
your address would be entirely up to you. Most of our guests opt to
speak after the main course, but more than one has opted to speak
before dinner, on the grounds that this makes the meal more
enjoyable. The choice is yours.

I hope you can make space in your diary for the Exeter Round Table.
I know you will rarely find a more appreciative audience.

Yours sincerely,

Michael Hunt
Speaker Co-ordinator

The flattery is implicit, rather than effusive. Mr Moore is offered the opportunity to address a tame, receptive audience, to arrange the schedule to suit himself (and his wife), and to be entertained in some style. Why should he refuse?

➡ DIRECT MAILSHOTS

There are as many reasons for writing direct mail letters and publications as there are businesses and organisations. There are also publications that deal with what is a highly specialised field beyond the scope of this book.

As the normal response to most direct mailings is between 1.5 per cent and 2 per cent, it is not normally a cost-effective option for small-to-medium-sized enterprises. The main advantage is that your organisation will get to invididuals and businesses who would not otherwise have heard of you. You never know when your expertise might be needed.

A few principles will help anyone wanting to try direct mail:

- Find out as much about your potential clients/supporters as possible. The wide availability of cross-referenced mailing lists makes it easy to select your target audience.
- Tailor your message to the particular client group. Sending out a letter or leaflet extolling the virtues of your organisation without recognising your readers' concerns will almost certainly ensure

that your mailing goes straight in the bin.
- Keep your information simple. Pages of detailed explanation and reasons why the reader should buy/support/subscribe to your business will only put off potential clients. Select a few key phrases, and hammer them home.

The following is an excellent example of targeted direct mail, from an insurance company that bought Amnesty International's mailing list with the aim of opening up a new market:

Dear Ms Smith,

We would like to offer you the chance to take out home insurance with [*name*] – and at the same time benefit Amnesty International. As a company, we are conscious of our obligations to society at large, and as a result have entered into an agreement with Amnesty International to donate £10 for every new policy taken out by their members.

If you are interested in this offer, please contact us to discuss your needs and to enable us to offer you a quote. If you currently have home insurance and wish to change to [*name*], your new policy will be arranged to run from the date that your previous policy ends.

The offer of a positive benefit to an organisation that the reader already supports is a powerful inducement. It gives the impression that the company has done its homework, and that, in an industry not renowned for its altruism, it has a social conscience too. It certainly worked for one of this book's co-authors, even managing to reduce annual premiums in the process! If the letter had begun with laborious detail about the type of policy available and only mentioned the donation to Amnesty International in the last paragraph, it would probably not have worked. By mentioning Amnesty in the first sentence, it immediately struck a chord.

This lesson can be applied to every sort of business, whether it's a small firm putting cards through letterboxes or a major multinational company embarking on a global marketing strategy. Before picking up a pen or sitting down in front of a word processor, business writers should ask themselves 'How can I best strike a chord with my target audience?'

Direct mail experts offer potential customers some incentives to respond. Good examples are the book and music clubs, which offer six books or CDs for 50 pence each if you subscribe and agree to buy a certain number of books or CDs in a year. They make their envelopes look as important and enticing as possible. They don't waste time with phrases like 'I'm sorry to bother you, but . . .' (an immediate turn off – why write at all if you're sorry about it?); or 'As you know, Brown's Threads are market leaders . . .' (So what?); or 'You know you won't regret taking up this offer . . .' (which has the reader wondering what the catch is). They are, instead, invariably simple and direct, while ensuring that potential customers feel wanted. And they are not afraid to repeat the message to make sure it hits home:

Strong's Tax Advice Service – saving you money; saving you stress

0112-333444

The Taxpayer
20 Park View
Edinburgh
EH6 2BZ

3 May 1999

Dear Taxpayer

Saving you money; saving you stress

Does the thought of your annual tax return give you nightmares? You'll sleep more easily if you take advantage of my introductory offer to take care of your annual returns for one-third of my normal price. All you need to do is phone me on the above number, and I'll arrange to come round to see you. I offer a completely confidential, 100% reliable service that is used by more than 200 people per year.

I look forward to hearing from you.

Yours faithfully

Sam Strong

PS. Remember – Strong's Tax Advice Service saves you money and saves you stress.

➡ YOUR AIM IN MARKETING

Whether you're producing a little card to put through letterboxes or a full-page advertisement in a national newspaper, you need to remember a few principles:

- Decide your core message – what are you selling and why?
- Research your audience – what do they want?
- Get to the point as quickly as possible.
- Use clear language and short sentences, without jargon.
- Make your customers feel wanted.

Chapter 8
Organising your writing

In the age of the Internet, when there's never been so much accessible data – or so much superfluous verbiage – what people need, above all, is well ordered information. In this chapter we shall consider how to gather, filter, arrange and present written material.

The principles of organising information are much the same as those for arranging words in a sentence, discussed in Part 1. We need to arrange material in the right order, so that readers can breathe, see what is coming, and follow a line of reasoning.

➡ LISTING ITEMS

Apart from putting things in the right order, one of the commonest ways of organising information in writing is to create lists. There are plenty in this book. Like conversational writing, lists are attractive because they reflect real life. We all make lists, whether for shopping, for daily tasks, for party guests or for fantasy sport teams.

One of the reasons that these lists are useful is that they are usually lists of similar things – food, household goods, or names of people – and are easy to follow. If you were asked to go shopping and were given a list varying from baking soda to pairs of socks and electrical equipment, it would be much more difficult.

The problem with a lot of business writing is that people start a list, then think of something else that doesn't really belong, and try to stuff it in the list anyway. Consider this internal memo:

The brochure will contain an application form lasered with: customer's name, address, account number, NI number and to include interest rates.

The reader gets to the end, and immediately has to read the sentence again. One moment the writer was listing customer details; then he switched to interest rates – simply because he had forgotten to put them in the right place. That paragraph should have read:

The brochure will give details of current interest rates. It will also contain an application form lasered with the customer's name, address, account number and National Insurance number.

Now it makes sense; we've got the interest rates out of the way, and gone on to list the customer's personal details that are lasered onto the application form.

Now let's look at a list in the form of bullet points. For example:

We have

- introduced a new management structure
- assessed the scope for further acquisitions
- started to decentralise responsibilities.

That's clear enough, isn't it? It is a list of actions taken. But in its original form, it read:

Much has been achieved already:

- *the introduction of a new management structure*
- *assessing the scope for further acquisitions*
- *the first steps have been taken to decentralise responsibilities*

This is hopelessly confusing. The writer has not bothered to compile the list properly, and we move from a noun in the first bullet point to an entire sentence as the third and final point. The revised version, by beginning each point with a verb, provides clarity and consistency.

There is one other thing to remember about bullet points. They are used to break up a page of normal paragraphs, to stand out and be memorable. Yet some people in business have become so addicted to bullet points that they insist on writing entire pages of them. This completely defeats the object. In a page of bullet points, a single normal paragraph would be the part to stand out. Besides, readers can only remember short lists, so there is never any point in listing more than six items in bullet points. Please check the lists and bullet points in this book, and let us know if we have departed from our own strictures.

➡ WRITING REPORTS

Now we come to reports – by which we mean anything that is too weighty or detailed for a letter, memo, fax or e-mail. For our purposes, all of the following can be treated as reports: minutes and meeting reports; sales proposals; feasibility studies; progress reports; instruction manuals; and annual reports.

Winston Churchill had the right approach to report-writing:

> To do our work, we all have to read a mass of papers. Nearly all of them are far too long. This wastes time, while energy has to be spent in looking for the essential points.
>
> The aim should be reports which set out the main points in a series of short, crisp paragraphs. If a report relies on detailed analysis of some complicated factors, or on statistics, these should be set out in an Appendix. Often the occasion is best addressed by submitting not a full-dress report, but an *aide-mémoire* consisting of headings only, which can be expanded orally if needed.
>
> Let us have an end of such phrases as these: 'It is also of importance to bear in mind the following considerations' or 'Consideration should be given to the possibility of carrying into effect'. Most of these woolly phrases are mere padding, which can be left out altogether or replaced by a single word. Let us not shrink from using the short, expressive phrase, even if it is conversational.
>
> Reports drawn up on the lines I propose may at first seem rough as

compared with the flat surface of officialese jargon. But the saving in time will be great, while the discipline of setting out the real points concisely will prove an aid to clear thinking.

Brevity (a Memo to the War Cabinet, 9 August 1940)

Isn't it amazing how apposite these words seem almost 60 years later?

Before you start to write, ask yourself if you need a document as complicated as a report. Far too many businesses produce long, boring publications that are never actually read, or are read by only two or three people, when a short leaflet, or even two well laid-out sides of A4, would have reached many more people and made much more impact.

If you are convinced you need to produce a report, ask yourself these vital questions:

- What is it for?
- Who is it for?
- What should it say?
- How should it say it?

Once you have produced a first draft, you should then consider two further questions:

- How does the report look?
- Does it read well?

What is it for?

As with every writing task, the first priority is to know your purpose. If your aim is to sell something, you should probably be concentrating on the product, not the company. If you are reporting back on something, make it as concise as possible. If you are taking the minutes of a meeting, accuracy should be your prime concern.

Short reports don't need much organisation, but longer documents – anything over four or five pages – must be carefully structured, from the title and list of contents right through to the conclusions, appendix, and maybe even a glossary, bibliography or list of sources at the end. You need to know the scale of your task from the beginning, and so if you're not sure what is required, ask your boss, or client, or whoever is commissioning you.

With a research report or progress report, you are usually telling interested readers what you have discovered and why it matters. You may also want to include a description of your methodology and your sources – the information's weight and reliability may depend where it comes from. The cost of the project, too, is likely to be of great interest. If there's a specific problem, you can state it clearly in the form of a question. And always, you will be trying to point out where your research is leading.

This is even more the case with a feasibility study or a report with recommendations, in which the conclusions or recommendations are paramount. Should we go ahead with whatever it is? In a report of this kind, you are essentially making a case for a particular course of action (or inaction). The report should be structured with this constantly in mind.

Keepers of minutes and meeting reports are expected to provide a true record of proceedings. Hansard's parliamentary reports, for instance, have a clear principle of accuracy, which nevertheless doesn't mean an absolutely literal record of every word spoken. MPs, like most people, fluff their lines from time to time, and Hansard will not compound their embarrassment by recording every slip or malapropism. Nor will Hansard pay any attention to interruptions from the public gallery – they are not part of the House's proceedings!

With management meetings, you can probably be more concise. The main value of minutes or meeting reports is to keep a record of decisions and to remind people what they agreed to do. Endless paragraphs recording what everyone said aren't necessary.

Annual reports or other periodic reviews record what has happened in the past period. But they are not entirely objective. They are intended to reassure shareholders and impress potential clients and the public. As the main vehicle for showing off what your organisation has achieved in the past year, the annual report is largely a selling document and needs to be planned accordingly.

Who is it for?

Too many people approach report-writing self-consciously. They write to impress or justify themselves. And they write about the things that interest them, rather than the things that might interest their readers. If you really want to impress the people who are going to read your report, you need to think about them, and what they want and expect.

This means putting yourself in their position, using language they will understand, and signposting sections for their benefit. Try thinking of yourself as a barrister, making constant appeals to the jury. Your readers are your jury, and if you make a real effort to guide them through your report, you will be more likely to win their support.

Nowhere is this more relevant than in a sales proposal. Here, everything must lead towards a single conclusion. You need to assemble all the evidence that would convince a potential customer to do business with you: relevant case studies, testimonials from satisfied customers, a pricing package to make it attractive to this particular client, plus perhaps some warning of dire consequences if they do not take specific action. Make it look good – perhaps by including photographs. Above all, you need to demonstrate that you understand the reader's position and that you are addressing their particular problems. Be careful not to overstate these problems; just state them as they have been explained to you. Then offer a solution as closely tailored to their situation as possible.

Instruction manuals provide many classic examples of complete lack of reader awareness. Perhaps you remember the table-assembly instructions from an earlier chapter. Here is another example of how not to do it from the 'Instructions for use' with antihistamine nose drops:

Uses
These nasal drops are indicated for the prophylactic treatment of allergic rhinitis (seasonal and perennial).

Directions for use
Since therapy with the nasal drops is essentially prophylactic, it is important to maintain regular dosage, as distinct from using the drug

intermittently to relieve symptoms. Adults and children: Instil two drops into each nostril six times daily, or as directed by your doctor.

Contraindications
These nasal drops are contraindicated in patients with known hypersensitivity to any of the constituents of the formulation. The constituents are sodium cromoglycate, sodium edetate, benzalkonium chloride and purified water.
© Plain English Campaign

All that these instructions are saying is: (a) the drops are for hay fever; (b) dosage is two drops six times a day or on a doctor's instructions; and (c) if users find they are allergic to the drops, they should stop taking them.

If you want people to read your instructions, write them in plain English. Of course you can't be sure about the level of intelligence and the training of your readers, so it may be difficult to find a balance between stating the obvious and being patronising. In general, though, a few key rules are as follows:

- Assume maximum ignorance on the part of the reader.
- Use simple words, preferably accompanied by illustrations.
- Use step-by-step instructions.
- Include a helpline phone number.

You should never forget the look of your report. Can you break up the text with photographs, graphics, tables and lists? Remember the presentational tools discussed in Chapter 4. Research reports should almost certainly include some tables or graphs, not just for presentation but to reinforce the main text.

For other types of report, you can work out who your readers are by doing a simple exercise: write down the names and professions of people you want to read your report. Think about the types of report you've had from *them*. What were they like? Have they worked? Did you read them? If they weren't successful, ask yourself why not. Too many words? Not enough graphics? Boring articles? No clear idea of the report's direction? Make notes and keep them as an *aide-mémoire*.

If other people's reports *do* succeed, decide what it was that appealed and try to imitate it. It may take some practice, but by the time you've learnt to write in the same way as authors you admire, you'll be ready to produce good writing using your own voice. And you'll appeal to the right readers.

What should it say?

Now you've decided what your report is aiming to achieve, and who is likely to read it, it's time to work out what to put in it. It sometimes helps to write down everything you want to include, and then try to arrange that into a structure. Above all, work out what the overriding message of your report should be.

One way of doing this is to write a summary. A one-page executive or management summary is an increasingly popular method for getting your message across to busy executives who might not read the full report. If you try to produce a summary early on, you can always change it later, although some people habitually prefer to leave it to the end. The summary should contain:

- a brief description of the purpose of the report
- the key issues, probably in bullet points
- the main recommendations.

Once you have assembled all the information you need, sift through it and decide what is important and what isn't. With an annual report, for instance, your first instinct might be to include everything your organisation has done in the past year. But there is no way people will read it all. They will pick out the little bits they know about or that appeal to them, but most of it will remain unread. Concentrate, therefore on the key events of the year and the people involved.

Use highlighter pens on your report summary to organise what belongs with each subject heading, such as:

- terms of reference/objectives
- introduction/background
- meetings
- present situation

- assessment of options
- findings
- cost
- recommendations/conclusions
- appendices.

Number the paragraphs as they relate to each of your sections. You may find that you have got dozens of paragraphs for the middle sections and relatively few for the introductions and conclusions. That's the wrong balance: the most important element of any report is the introduction, which encourages the reader to read on, and the conclusion, which – if clear enough – saves the reader from having to study the middle section. Look at what you've written and work out what would be stronger in the introduction than in the middle. Then look at what should be in the conclusion.

Once the content of the introduction is clear, and you know the conclusion (usually a distillation of the main discussion), look at all the other elements you need to include. In an annual report, for instance, these might be:

- the strategic objectives of the organisation
- the geographical areas where it works
- the projects it supports
- the main achievements of the past year
- financial information
- employee issues
- environment and community issues.

How should it say it?

Now that you have assembled and sifted everything that is relevant to your report, it's time to write the first draft, keeping as closely as possible to the structure you have chosen.

Title
The title says what the report is about – and as simply as possible. Short reports only need a title; longer reports often have a title and

sub-title (e.g. *The Liberal Challenge: Democracy as Participation*). The author's name and date should also be on the title page if appropriate.

Don't spend ages trying to work out the best title. If you find it difficult, just write down a working title. You can always come back to it later.

Contents list
Only long reports need a contents list, which should be on a separate page and give all the section headings plus, if appropriate, sub-headings. Each section and sub-section may be numbered, in Civil Service fashion. If the report is for an internal audience, this can be useful when it comes to discussing particular paragraphs. But if the report is for public consumption, avoid numbered paragraphs, which look officious.

Summary (often called Executive Summary)
The summary usually comes at the beginning of a report, to enable readers to grasp the main contents without reading the whole thing. We dealt with this in the last section.

Introduction/Objectives/Terms of Reference
This section should be short, and explain:

- the purpose of the report
- the background to the report
- who the report is for
- how the work was done
- what it cost (if relevant)
- any acknowledgements.

You only have a limited time to get each reader's attention (remember the average reader has a 15-second attention span) and convince them to read on. So it's worth making a special effort to get the introduction right.

Don't clutter your opening with a lot of technical detail. Explain anything the title might not make clear, especially if it's an abstract title. You could do worse than begin by saying 'This report is about . . .' The rest of the section should explain why it is worth reading.

The body of the report

The middle sections will be the densest, covering such subjects as the story so far, descriptions, meetings, discussions, key issues, analysis, findings, etc. The mass of information is here, and it is up to you to make it as digestible as possible.

Face the fact that very few readers will read every word of the discussion (in the same way that almost nobody reads a newspaper or magazine from cover to cover), and so break the material down into as many headings and sub-headings as is sensible. Start each section with the most important points. The same applies to the paragraphs: put the key point in the first sentence before adding the detail.

Conclusions/Recommendations

Sometimes these are separate sections – it depends on your original brief, and where your report leads you. You may like to explain your conclusions, then devote a separate section to your recommendations. Alternatively your brief may only invite you to draw conclusions, but not to make recommendations. Or you may decide that it is easier to wrap up the report in one section, summarising the steps you think should be taken as a result of the work described in the report.

Use bullet points and keep paragraphs short. Don't include everything you've put in the report; highlight the important actions you believe are required.

Appendices

If you think a particular issue or case study worth exploring, but don't want to interrupt the flow of the report, you may choose to put it in an appendix.

Appendices are useful if you come to an important technical matter that cannot readily be explained for the lay reader. Then those with the necessary technical knowledge can turn to the appendix for the detail that they will appreciate.

How does it look, and does it read well?

These are the last vital questions. Once you've written your first draft, leave it overnight at least. Maybe show it to a trusted colleague. The next time you look at it, you want to be looking with a fresh eye, approaching it for the first time as a reader.

You may find that your headings don't work; if so, change them – and rearrange the information as necessary. Make sure the report is accessible and flows logically.

Check for points at which you might have got too technical – *you* may know what 'instantiation' means, but your readers almost certainly will not. And have you used acronyms or sets of initials that are familiar to you but not necessarily to every reader of the report? It's easy to forget that the language used daily in your business is a mystery to the rest of the world.

Check on the look of the report. Have you included enough quotes, graphs and tables to break up the text, and to reinforce your argument?

Have another look at the title and see if you could make it more interesting or memorable, perhaps by choosing a punchy title, with an explanatory sub-title. *The Merits of Developing Computer Technology for Village Schools in Third World Countries* doesn't have the same impact as *IT for All* with a sub-title of *Developing Computers for Developing Countries*.

In this age of IT and word processing, it's possible to play around with your text to get an idea of how it will look in various different formats. Big corporate reports will be put out to professional designers, but reports designed for in-house use can be word processed and stapled without any problem.

Other issues to consider at this stage are:

- acknowledgements – are there any people you should thank?
- footnotes and bibliography
- a glossary, especially if you've used a lot of technical terms
- a covering letter – does the report need explanation?

Once you're happy with the layout and the words, double-check with all the relevant people – few employers appreciate having to reprint documents that have been sent out with mistakes in them.

If there is any danger of legal complications, ask a lawyer to check it *before* you send it out.

You should have decided your readership before you started writing, but it's always worth looking carefully at your mailing list. Other names or organisations might have occurred to you during the writing. If you've done a good job, you want as many people as possible to appreciate it!

Chapter 9
Electronic mail

➡ WHY USE ELECTRONIC MAIL?

Electronic mail (e-mail) has become a fact of life for many people in business – and many in private life as well. Over 55 million people are already using it worldwide and the number increases every day. Suddenly we can all communicate with each other without having to write letters that need to be posted, opened, read and filed; without picking up the phone and possibly intruding into meetings or conversations; without having to talk to other people face to face.

E-mail is quick, convenient, and in many ways harks back a few hundred years to the days when people exchanged several letters in the space of one day: communication by the written word rather than person to person. E-mail has reintroduced the art of conversation by letter, which was rapidly becoming a lost skill.

The great benefit of e-mail is that you can communicate with people worldwide at the strike of a few keys, and without having to worry about time zones. You can say what you want when the idea first occurs, type in your thoughts, follow through your ideas and express your concerns, all in the privacy of your own computer – and then send the message spinning round the world, where it will sit in the recipient's mailbox waiting to be read. Instead of the cut and thrust of face-to-face conversation or the risk of interrupting a phone call or a meeting, the e-mail waits quietly to be dealt with in the recipient's own time. It allows time for measured reactions.

For busy business executives, this is an enormous advantage and removes the need to spend a lot of time on the telephone or travelling to meetings. With most e-mail systems, telephone call time is charged at the local rate.

The electronic mailbox has become as important to many people as the front-door letter-box. It has benefits for both businesses and their clients. Internal office e-mail cuts down time spent wandering through departments and chatting to people, at the same time as speeding up the communication process. External e-mail means you can update clients and colleagues at home and abroad in minutes and send them news and briefings; and they can ask you crucial questions even if you're half a world away. Any computer-literate executive can use e-mail after very brief training.

Electronic mail is a good way of ensuring spontaneous communication: unlike letters which are often edited and amended, e-mails tend to be sent as soon as they are written.

Electronic mail has many advantages:

- It is spontaneous, and tends to reflect immediate thoughts.
- It goes anywhere in the world at the cost of a local phone call.
- It cuts out the risks of interruption.
- It reduces the need for meetings.
- It saves time and money.

➡ CREATING AN E-MAIL MESSAGE

Using your electronic address book

The first challenge of e-mail is to make sure you get the recipient's address right. It's very easy to think you've typed the right sequence of words and punctuation, only to find your e-mail whizzing back to you with the message 'recipient unknown at that address'. Regular users of e-mail keep electronic address books, in which the names of contacts and their e-mail addresses are recorded. Every time you want to send a message to an e-mail contact, you go into your address book (at the section sometimes known as 'Nicknames' or 'Address Book'), click on the person's name, click on 'To:' and the name appears automatically at the top of the e-mail overleaf.

You can also record groups of people under one name. Say, for example, that you are a member of a choir. You can generally file the name 'choir' in the address book, and type in the e-mail addresses of all the members in an associated section. You then apply the same process as before when starting a new message: choose 'choir' as the addressee and your message will be sent to all the members.

A sample address book could look like that shown in Figure 9.1 – this is the one on the Eudora system. Other systems may vary but the principle is the same:

Contacts	Address(es)	
Choir	mary.brown@mat.org.uk jbowers@compuserve.com hsmith@ukonline.co.uk suttiep@virgin.net	To CC BCC

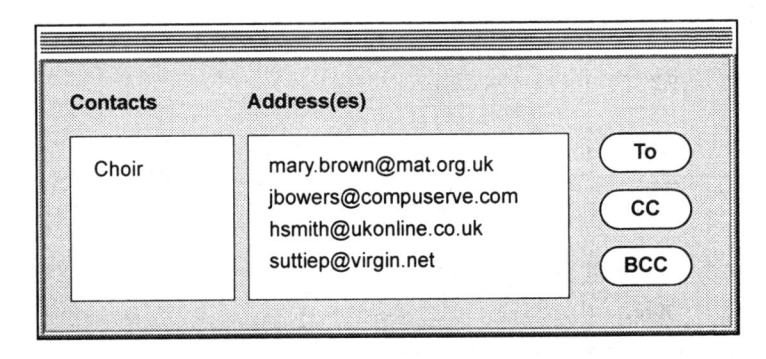

Figure 9.1: Simulated screen for an electronic address book

If you then want the same message to go to someone else who is not on the choir list, click on that person's name in the address book then click on 'CC:' and their name will appear next to CC: in the message. Don't be concerned that their e-mail address doesn't come up – it's logged in the system, and will show up on all the recipients' messages. As a result, everyone will know who has been sent the information.

A sample outgoing e-mail created in this way would look like that shown in Figure 9.2.

To	Choir
From	david@sparks.co.uk
Subject	Next committee meeting
CC	peter
BCC	
Attachments	c:\choir\mins3.doc

Figure 9.2: Simulated e-mail message header (as sent)

The recipients' e-mails would appear as shown in Figure 9.3.

From	david@sparks.co.uk
X-real-To	mary.brown@mat.org.uk
Date	29 September 1998
Subject	Next committee meeting
To	jbowers@compuserve.com, hsmith@ukonline.co.uk, suttiep@virgin.net
cc	peterj@bcc.com
Attachments	c:\eudora\apps\mins3.doc

Figure 9.3: Simulated e-mail message header (as received)

Subjects and attachments

The subject line of an e-mail message is important because busy people get dozens of messages every day; by making the subject clear, you give them the chance to decide whether or not an e-mail is urgent. Furthermore, you can flag up urgent e-mails by going into your system's equivalent of an 'options' box in the message window.

There is no point in writing a long document in an e-mail message: e-mail is typographically still very simple, and can't deal with large quantities – or variable formats – of text. When you print out an e-mail, sentences often break up into odd clumps, and it can be hard to make sense of them. So when you have something more complicated to send by e-mail, use the attachment facility.

This facility is one of the biggest benefits of electronic mail but its operation is too specialist for this book to address. It allows you to send long, detailed reports over the telephone line without having to go to the trouble and expense of faxing or posting them. It also allows the recipient to respond more quickly and, if necessary, make any changes they want before sending it back.

➡ WRITING EFFECTIVE E-MAIL

Electronic mail is developing a language and conventions all of its own. Because the software only allows for the most basic text, it encourages streams of thought. Even writing 'Dear...' at the beginning is going out of fashion, and some people don't bother with any salutation, allowing the 'To:' and 'Subject:' to say it all.

It's an informal system, which encourages the spontaneous sharing of ideas. But that's no reason to start writing badly. Unfortunately, many people use it as if it were a scribbled note, full of spelling mistakes and without any proper punctuation.

That's fine if it's a chatty note to a friend or colleague passing on a piece of information:

> Jane,
>
> I can come over tomorrow to sign the cheques - won't be before 2.30 - hope that's OK.
>
> David

It encourages informality and promotes genuine communication. It also allows people to get messages across without any barriers. But it's important that more formal messages to business colleagues and partners are written more or less properly:

> John,
>
> When we spoke last week, you asked me to find out some information about marketing in Brazil. By chance I ran into someone last night who works for Butler & Groves, which has a branch out there. I've asked him to get in touch with you. Hope it works out – it's a fascinating country.
>
> See you, Diana

This is less formal than a letter would be, but gets the message across clearly and concisely. The informality of e-mail allows you to sign off in a more relaxed way.

The principles of clarity, short words, grammar and punctuation apply to e-mail as much as to any other form of writing. There's no need to lose the conversational tone; but remember that many e-mails are printed out, and something that looks chatty and informal on screen may seem overfamiliar on paper.

It's particularly important if you are e-mailing someone whom you don't know very well. Ask yourself: What will the reader think? What reaction do I want? What should I – and shouldn't I – say? Apply the same criteria as you would to a letter – after all, the chances are that the message will be printed out.

Imagine that a prospective client has asked you to develop a marketing strategy for a new product – a self-descaling kettle. You've been given all the information and asked to come up with an outline plan after you've consulted colleagues. You think it will take three days, and you want to charge £3,000. A model e-mail could read:

```
From:     julia.smithson@smithson.co.uk
To:       petermcd@superk.co.uk
Subject:  Self-descaling kettle
```

Dear Peter

Thank you for all the material about the Super Kettle. We are very enthusiastic, and would like to help make it a success.

You asked me to give you an estimate of the cost of producing a marketing strategy. I would be able to start work on it next week and could have a document ready for you by the following Monday. We think it will take three days to produce a detailed plan including ideas, a range of options and an accurately costed budget. This would come to £3,000 - less than the market rate, but we reckon the product is so marketable that we're willing to take the risk.

I've already tried the idea out on some colleagues, and they think it's brilliant.

With best wishes, Julia

This is, in effect, an electronic letter, which reads well and addresses the issues – but the temptation of e-mail could easily lead you to dash off something quite different:

```
From:     julia.smithson@smithson.co.uk
To:       petermcd@superk.co.uk
Subject:  Self-descaling kettle
```

Peter

I've read through your stuff and we think it's great. We'll do the plan for you for £3,000 (cheap at twice the price) and have it for you by next week.

Cheers, Julia

It all depends on the rapport you have established with the recipient. This gets across the basic message, but could easily come across as hurried and slapdash. Overall, it is not as convincing or reassuring as the longer, more measured message.

When writing email messages:

- apply the principles of good writing
- be as brief as possible
- use a tone appropriate for the reader
- be clear.

Further hints for good e-mails

E-mail is not a word-processing package with all the twiddles and ornamentations available. It is a very basic system. There are only basic typefaces and no underlining, emboldening, italic or indentation. And generally at present there is no spellchecker.

Because it's such an immediate medium, many people don't bother to read over what they've written. As a result, hundreds of badly spelt and unpunctuated messages fly through the aether every day. This doesn't matter if you're chatting to friends, but it does for business communications. Its immediacy is its appeal, but that doesn't mean you shouldn't read it through before you send it.

Another problem is margins. Many systems don't seem to have any, so when you print something out it falls off the edge of the page. This is only one of the hazards involved in using e-mail! Use the space bar to ensure that you have wide margins.

The language of e-mail is changing all the time. Formality is out; slang (but not jargon) is in. New uses of letters and symbols are also popular – there's a school of thought that thinks if you don't know how to use a 'Smiley', you aren't with it. A 'Smiley' is a device that lets the reader know how you feel about something – usually made up of brackets and punctuation marks. For example, if you're pleased about something, type colon dash close bracket :-), which your word-processing system may well convert to ☺; if you're unhappy, type colon dash open bracket :-(, which may be converted to ☹; and if you want to be ironic, type semi-colon dash close bracket ;-). There are hundreds of variations on these.

A few concluding hints:

- Use email for sharing ideas and asking questions.
- Read it through before you click the 'send' button.
- Keep messages short, to the point and factual.
- Don't use e-mail for long communications, except by using file attachments.

➡ THE PERILS OF E-MAIL

Of course the system isn't perfect, and security can be a problem. Unless your message is encrypted, it can be intercepted. However, your supplier should be able to tell you how to make messages more secure.

Another difficulty is reliability – or lack of it. With hundreds of new users coming onto the Internet every day, systems can get gummed up, e-mail operators can fail, messages can go astray, and server computers can break down. The worst problems usually happen when you're setting a system up for the first time – again, refer any problems to your service provider.

We've written earlier in the book about the advantages of spontaneity, but it can have a down side. It's easy to write something and press the 'send' key before you've either read or thought through what you've written – and once it's gone, you can't get it back. Always read your messages and make sure they really say what you mean.

There's also the possibility of plagiarising other people's information – the electronic medium makes it so easy to recycle information, that you can never be quite sure where something will end up.

But in general, electronic mail is an advantage to business, allowing busy people to save time and money and to speed up national and international communications.

Use it. Enjoy it.

Chapter 10
Corporate Writing Disease

When people write on behalf of their company, or in any sort of business contact, they find it hard to be themselves. All too often, they seem to become afflicted by some highly infectious bug that makes them use a language quite alien from everyday English. These are some of its manifestations.

- pomposity
- verbosity
- tautology
- obfuscation
- nounitis
- jargon.

One thing that all these afflictions have in common is that they produce language designed to impress, not inform. It is sometimes known as 'management-speak'. We call it Corporate Writing Disease (CWD). Whatever you call it, it is the kind of language that creates a gulf of distrust between writer and reader. Yet throughout the business world, enlightened executives know the value of speaking the customer's language and communicating in plain English.

The following example from an NHS circular is an extreme example of corporate pomposity taking over public life.

BED

A device or arrangement that may be used to permit a patient to lie

> *down when the need to do so is a consequence of the patient's condition rather than a need for active intervention, diagnostic investigation, manipulative treatment, obstetric delivery or transport.*
>
> *Beds, couches or trolleys are also counted as hospital beds where:*
>
> - *used regularly as a means of support for patients needing a lengthy procedure such as renal dialysis*
> - *used regularly to allow patients to lie down after sedation.*
>
> *NB A device specifically and solely for the purpose of delivery should not be counted as a bed.* [©Plain English Campaign]

Corporate writing disease particularly afflicts companies under pressure. Rather than tackle the questioning or complaint head-on, they lapse into defensive language and unnecessarily complicated sentences. This paragraph comes from a building society's response to a gentle letter of complaint about late payment of interest:

> *In so far as it is within our abilities to ensure that our clients receive interest on the pre-arranged date, we do so. Unfortunately in the two months to which you refer in your letter the society was undergoing a profound process of change and development. As a result, certain of our regular activities became caught up in the cycle of change which led to some diminuition in our service.*

Why didn't they just say they were sorry for the delay, which was the result of internal changes? The use of words and phrases like 'In so far as it is' 'profound process of change and development' and 'diminution in our service' are management-speak used to hide the fact that they slipped up. Customers and clients who receive these kinds of letters become annoyed and feel alienated. They do not feel that the building society is genuinely sorry.

There is no single style of CWD, but banks can usually be relied upon:

> *If for any reason you are unable to provide immediate funds to adjust the position . . .*

which means, simply:

> If you cannot pay any money in . . .

This is what real people do: they pay money into their accounts and they draw money out. Yet many banks still insist on 'remitting funds' or 'withdrawing monies'.

The next example comes from that reliable source of bad corporate writing, local government. This particular sample has become a staple for teachers of good writing:

> *Your enquiry gives rise to the question of the provenance and authoritativeness of the material to be displayed. All items of a disputatious or polemic kind, while not necessarily excluded, are considered individually.*

Not content with being alarmingly illiberal, it also uses vocabulary more suited to an academic treatise. And all it means is that the local authority needs to check the text of all leaflets displayed publicly in their buildings.

Finally, in this section, an example of CWD from an instruction manual:

VERSION A

> *In the event of any failure or malfunctioning of any component of the apparatus which renders the appliance inoperative and necessitates repair before the appliance will work normally, the company will, at the request of the customer within a reasonable period and during normal working hours, repair or replace such components free of charge.*

Or in plain English:

VERSION B

> If the appliance breaks down due to a faulty part, please let us know. We will then repair or replace the part free of charge within a reasonable time during normal working hours. [© Plain English Campaign]

The effect is much clearer, and gives an impression of efficiency and competence that reflects well on the company.

➡ WAFFLE – TAUTOLOGY AND VERBOSITY

Tautology literally means 'saying the same thing'. It is a convenient way of filling up empty space for the verbose writer – you use words and phrases and then write them again in a different way. 'Space prevents us translating the entire article, which would run to several columns' is a tautological sentence, because the writer has already explained that space is a problem and there is no need to add to that explanation.

Another commonly used phrase 'in conjunction with each other' is also tautological: if you're in conjunction, you must be with someone else. Equally woolly is the insertion of unnecessary words. 'Work is required to be carried out on the toilets and fittings' doesn't need 'to be carried out'. 'For the benefit of new members of the group, the Secretary described the remit given to it' is similarly long-winded. An improvement would be: 'For the benefit of new members, the Secretary described the group's remit.'

Straightforward repetition is a surprisingly common habit that should be cured by a simple read-through:

The cheque that was received from Greengrass Insurance was received on 23 September.

This sort of repetition is even more irritating:

Dear Mr Smithers

Joe Bloggs caretakers – assessment and appraisal of their work Monday 23 July 1997, Little Brough School

This is to confirm that an assessment and appraisal of the work of Joe Bloggs caretakers will take place on Monday 23 July 1997 at Little Brough School.

I confirm that all the arrangements are in place.

Yours sincerely

Why confirm twice what you've already mentioned in a heading? Much better to write:

Dear Mr Smithers

Joe Bloggs caretakers – assessment and appraisal of their work
Monday 23 July 1997, Little Brough School

We have completed all the arrangements for the above assessment and look forward to seeing you there.

Yours sincerely

Verbosity can be a result of trying too hard to please:

I will make contact in the next few days to arrange a mutually convenient time to have a meeting.

As if you would arrange an inconvenient time! All you need is:

I will be in touch soon to arrange a meeting.

Avoiding repetition and waffle is a good discipline for a writer. And it proves that there is no substitute for reading everything through before you send it.

Another symptom of CWD is the use of long-winded phrases. Why use six words when one will do? The reason is usually because you are trying to sound important rather than communicate. Table 10.1 shows how to avoid common long-winded phrases.

Table 10.1: Ways to avoid long-windedness

Bad	**Good**
a sufficient quantity of	enough/plenty
as a consequence of	because
at the end of the day	eventually
at this point in time	now
avail yourself of	use
be cognisant of	know/be aware
despite the fact that	although/despite
for the duration of	during/while
in order to	to
increased by a factor of two	doubled

in the near future	soon/imminent
in view of the fact that	because/as
is capable of	can/is able to
in respect of	about
reiterate again	repeat
subsequent to	after
with reference to	about/concerning
on a daily basis	every day
on an individual basis	individually

➡ NOUNITIS

This word was coined by one of the co-authors to describe writing that uses too many nouns, another manifestation of CWD. The following examples highlight this tendency, with the nouns italicised and the verbs emboldened:

> The *reason* for the *success* of the new *product* **is** the *proliferation* of *people* **willing to promote** its usefulness to the *customer base*.

This style of writing, which uses eight nouns and only two verbs, attempts to mystify the simple process of getting people to go out and sell a product. It aims to make the reader feel awed by the cleverness of the marketing people. An alternative version, using only two nouns and four verbs, is shorter, clearer and more powerful:

> This *product* **is** successful because *people* **want** to **go** out and **sell** it.

Abstract nouns are a particular risk to healthy writing. They dull every sentence in which they appear, and they take the reader further away from real life. Here are a few examples:

- 'working environment' – do you mean 'office'?
- 'problematic situation' – surely just a 'problem'?
- 'customer base' – why not simply 'customers'?

- 'visitor resource' – surely they're 'visitors'?
- 'satisfaction level' – 'satisfaction'.
- 'weather conditions' – 'weather'.

Now have a look at a classic example of nounitis. This is the training manager of a bank writing to someone offering training courses – the nouns (23) and verbs (5) are again highlighted.

> At this *moment* in *time*, the *Bank* **continues** to **invest** heavily in *training* and *development initiatives* that **contribute** to the *advancement* of our challenging *business objectives*. The *development* of *employee potential* **is** a major *focus* of these *programmes*. Our *Leadership* and *Management Competence Training* **addresses** a very wide *range* of personal *management* and *leadership skills development*.

All this paragraph really means is: 'The bank already runs training courses for its staff,' and therefore we don't need your help, thank you very much. But instead of writing a nice, crisp letter thanking the trainer for his interest and promising to keep his name on file, the manager writes paragraphs of abstract and grandiose nonsense. What is the relevance of 'our challenging business objectives', whatever they might be? And what is training for if not for 'the development of employee potential'? Communication is clearly not the aim here. The writer has succumbed to CWD, and is using words to build a wall of self-justification around himself so that he can avoid confronting any real issues.

➡ EXAGGERATIONS

Exaggeration is one of the milder variants of CWD, but it is ultimately debilitating. When people load on the adjectives and adverbs to prove their sincerity, the effect is almost invariably the opposite.

If you say that a strategy was successful, that should be enough. But here are a few examples of unnecessary intensifiers:

- hugely successful
- deeply meaningful
- powerfully suggestive
- amazingly powerful
- fantastically seductive
- lyrically beautiful.

Each of the adjectives above carries weight in its own right – it doesn't need to be qualified by an adverb. These sorts of phrases are typical advertising-speak, but they also creep into business writing:

> It's been an action-packed ten years since the Biscuit Tin Corporation's first annual report. In those ten years, we have gone from being a tiny little one-man-and-a-dog operation to being an amazingly strong player in the biscuit-tin field. I can now very confidently predict that in another ten years we will be the leading providers of biscuit tins in Hopshire.

There are occasions when a bit of hyperbole does no harm, but if you write in a measured, reasoned way, you'll get a more positive response from your readers. If the Managing Director of the Biscuit Tin Corporation had written the following introduction, his clients and suppliers would have found it easier to recognise the firm's achievements – and known that he was being realistic about the future:

> Since the Biscuit Tin Corporation was established ten years ago, the company's turnover has increased sevenfold. Our clients rely on us, which leads me to hope that in another ten years the Corporation could be the leading provider in Hopshire.

➡ JARGON

Jargon is the bane of all good writers. As the world grows smaller and the use of English becomes universal, some phrases and words pass into the public domain without being challenged. A classic example is the 'level playing field'. Ten years ago no one knew what it meant; now it's used by everyone from the local school teacher to the heads of multinational corporations. But some jargon doesn't fit so comfortably into the language.

When you work in an area where you and all your colleagues and clients use the same phraseology, it's easy to fall into the habit of using words and phrases that mean nothing to the outside world. But if you want to write literature that has a wider appeal, it's important to examine your words and be careful not to blind general readers with jargon.

There are some jargon words that have become common, but it doesn't do any harm to remember that there are plain-English alternatives – some set out in Table 10.2. Most of these words are nouns, but where they are being used as verbs, we have put (v) afterwards.

Table 10.2: Ways to avoid jargon

Jargon	Plain English
parameters	boundaries/limits
optimum	best
feedback	response/reaction
entitlement	right
ring-fence	earmark/designate
relocate	move
prevalent	common
initiate	start
institute (v)	start
terminate (v)	finish
operational areas	areas of work
downsizing	redundancies/sackings
outplacements	redundancies/sackings
restructuring	redundancies/sackings
implement (v)	do/carry out
interface (v)	meet / discuss

finalise (v)	complete / finish
outputs	results / what you've achieved

➡ SUMMARY

CWD need not be the result of a deliberate wish to baffle the reader and make them feel that you are more important than them – but that's probably what will happen. Unless you are writing for a specialist reader who understands your references and your language, there is one rule:

Keep your words as simple as possible. Clarity is the soul of comprehension.

Chapter 11
Summary and conclusions

In case you haven't had the opportunity to read *Business Writing* from cover to cover, this chapter is for you. And for those of you who have read the book, it's a chance to refresh your memory.

➡ INTRODUCTION

Why bother with your writing? Because writing is an essential tool of communication and it's also part of the marketing process. Written material presents a company's image to the outside world. Well written memos, letters, reports and articles attract attention and inspire confidence; badly written ones go straight into the bin, undermining your business reputation in the process.

➡ CHAPTER 1: ASSESSING THE JOB

Whatever you are writing, you must first identify your purpose and your intended reader or readers. Then keep your message clear, concise and relevant.

Journalists are taught to write stories so that they draw the readers' attention to the first paragraph. Few people read an article from beginning to end, which is why journalists get the main story into the first few lines so the reader knows what it's about and can decide whether to read on into the detail. The same applies to business writing. Focus on the core message; the supporting information can come later.

You must always think about your reader. Once you've decided who is likely to read your message, put yourself in their shoes, then think how you would respond to what you are planning to write.

Business writing must be tailored to the clients' needs, not to yours. Officious language is a symptom of a failure to consider the reader.

➡ CHAPTER 2: ARRANGING THE WORDS – GRAMMAR

Learning to write is like learning to cook – you need the right ingredients before you can follow a recipe.

The basis of all writing is the sentence, a complete statement that can stand by itself. Average readable sentence length is between 15 and 25 words. You don't have to make every sentence the same length, but staying close to that number makes life easier for your reader. Don't write complicated sentences with passive, flowery words. Use short, punchy language; use the active voice.

Make the reader feel part of the writing. Use pronouns, not abstract nouns: 'we', 'you', 'they' rather than 'the company', 'the insurers', 'the bank'. 'We' suggests human beings; 'the bank' is something huge and impersonal.

Chapter 2 covers the details of grammar, including structure, subject/verb agreement, tenses and modifiers. The list summarises the basic tools for writing effective sentences:

- Write short, punchy sentences.
- Use active words.
- Use pronouns, not abstract nouns.
- Keep your sentences simple.
- Think about what your readers want to hear.

➡ CHAPTER 3: LISTENING TO THE WORDS – PUNCTUATION

Writing is conversation. It should have the same pauses, breaths and highs-and-lows as the words you speak.

Good writers listen to what they write; they imagine the words spoken aloud, and punctuate in their heads. The stresses and the quiet places should reflect the way the words should be spoken. If you start to read something out loud and realise that it's too convoluted to say smoothly, either you need to re-punctuate it or you're using too many words.

Good punctuation is not about rules; it's about helping the reader to pause – and concentrate – in the right places. Its aim is to make writing as close as possible to conversation. So listen to your words; read them out loud; punctuate accordingly.

Three things to remember are:

- Keep your writing conversational.
- Listen to your words.
- Punctuate for the reader's benefit.

➡ CHAPTER 4: LOOKING AT THE WORDS – LAYOUT

Good writing is about more than good use of language. It's about presenting your words in an attractive and eye-catching manner. Which would you rather read: a solid page of black type, or a page with headlines, sub-heads, an easy-to-read typeface and plenty of white space?

The advent of word processors has revolutionised writers's ability to influence the look of their work. Don't be put off by people who are able to produce beautifully designed documents at the touch of a few keys. Actually, anyone with a spare couple of hours can learn to enhance their words.

Choosing good layout is a matter of taste. Start by looking at documents in your office. Choose the ones you like best; work out why you like them. Make notes. Then choose the ones you like least and do the same. By now you should have some idea of the kind of layout you like.

There are three main elements to good layout:

- use of white space
- column width

- space between lines (leading)
- type style.

Columns should be narrow – the average reader's eye-span can absorb between 8 and 12 words in a column. Line spacing depends on the context – most letters and reports are single-spaced; articles and speeches tend to be 1.5 or double-spaced to allow for edits or insertions. Type-size and face is a matter of taste, but big blocks of text are more readable if they are broken up with headings and sub-headings.

People sometimes use CAPITAL LETTERS to emphasise or enhance their words. **Bold type** does the same job more neatly. Underlining is best for headings (if bold is not being used), although underlined words and phrases can clutter the page if used in the middle of text. *Italic* should only be used for quotations, titles or technical terms.

A word of warning – don't allow layout to detract from your words. It's tempting to get carried away with the design potential of technology. Try your ideas out on colleagues – if your layout has taken over from your words, you've gone too far. The main rules of layout can be summarised as:

- Use your technology.
- Think of your reader – how easy is the layout to read?
- Keep the design simple.
- Use the layout to complement, not distract from, your words.

➡ CHAPTER 5: WHAT'S THE FORM?

There are four preliminary questions to ask yourself if you want your writing to work:

- Do I need to write (as opposed to telephoning or calling in person), and if so, why?
- What sort of document is right for my target readership?
- What tone should I adopt?
- What should I include?

Once you've decided that you do need to write something, think about your readers and what kind of document is appropriate. If, for instance, you start out with a letter and find it is turning into a long document, you might consider writing a report with a covering note. Conversely, if your report can be summed up in one page, a memo will do – never be scared of being too brief. Ask yourself what *you* would expect to read on the subject.

Now you've chosen the vehicle, think about the content. Scribble down as many ideas as you can, and then refine them. What do you really want to say? What is the key message? How can you say it as clearly and simply as possible?

Basic rules for addressing people are laid out in Chapter 5. Be clear about who is the subject, and address them directly. Keep your language straightforward; avoid pomposity and verbosity; sign off politely.

When you come to the end of what you are writing, make sure you leave a clear impression. Be yourself. Don't use formulaic expressions such as 'If you have any further queries, please do not hesitate to call.' The most reliable sign-off is 'Yours sincerely'.

➡ CHAPTER 6: WRITING THAT WORKS

Applications and requests

Application letters – whether for a pension, to join a club or society, or for a job or pay rise – are personal. You need to strike the right balance between underselling and overselling yourself.

Make sure that you have all relevant information at your fingertips – there's no point in asking for a pension if you don't know how much you can afford to put aside; there's no point applying for a job if you don't have the right experience. Once you've got the information, be direct and straightforward: ask for what you want without covering it in flannel; explain honestly why you're the best person for the job.

Requests must explain exactly what you want or need to know. Mention the reason for the request at once, and if it involves a series of things, use lists and bullet points. And don't be scared to ask for advice or information.

When making a request or application:

- Find out everything you can about your readers, and what they want.
- Address all the essential criteria, or explain the crucial facts.
- Use every connection – references, recommendations, inducements – to make it personal.

Complaints and apologies

Letters of complaint should not be written in anger. These are the cardinal rules:

- State the facts as objectively as possible.
- Give the reader a chance to put things right.
- Threaten serious consequences if nothing is done.
- Keep the language restrained.

Letters of apology require even more sensitivity. But they can be well worth the effort, for if you can repair relations you can end up with the ideal – a customer whose loyalty will be long-term. Above all, you should try to see things from the complainer's point of view. These are the essential elements of an effective letter of apology:

- Address the customer's concerns directly.
- Apologise if necessary, but don't grovel.
- Explain what you are doing to put things right.
- Avoid arguing about details.

Introductions and references

Letters of introduction can range from a friendly note to a formal business letter. Here are a few tips:

- Mention the person's name in the first paragraph.
- Keep it personal.
- Keep it short.

With reference letters, you should:

- be sure you want to write the reference
- be honest
- answer all the potential employer's questions
- add a personal note.

Dismissals, rejections and resignations

Warning letters and dismissal letters must follow consistent guidelines, because one is liable to lead to the other. Consult a lawyer before committing yourself to paper.

With rejection letters it is worth taking time to explain your reasons and find something encouraging to say. You never know who the rejected person's friends might be!

Resignation should be

- explanatory
- friendly, unless you've had a major row
- written in such a way as to keep the door open for re-application or a reference.

Explanations and clarifications

Get the bad news out of the way first. Use neutral words such as 'misunderstanding' rather than judgmental words such as 'incorrect' or 'mistake'. Imagine you are talking to a close friend or relative and keep it as simple as possible.

➡ CHAPTER 7: WRITING THAT SELLS

Time is of the essence. You want to make an immediate impact on your potential customer, client or employer. You have to distinguish *your* product or service from anybody else's. And remember: the average attention span of someone reading a sales message is 15 seconds.

Before you start, decide the best way of putting your message across. Ask yourself:

- What is my unique selling point (USP)?
- What is my message?
- What is my medium?
- What can I offer the customer/client/employer?
- What would make me want to buy this product?

Try to think your way into your readers' minds before you start writing. Be objective, use simple language, engage them in the discussion.

Think about what you want to achieve, then choose the right vehicle. Whatever the vehicle, remember the three vital ingredients:

- a clear benefit the reader can instantly identify (a haircut, a fixed photocopier)
- a reason to choose this particular person (qualifications, testimonials)
- a deal-clincher – the reason to act now (a special offer, a personal recommendation).

Advertising

Use short words and sentences, amuse or challenge your readers, make the lay-out interesting – and don't forget to mention your name and how to get in touch.

Job applications

Research the organisation, read the job description carefully, follow the application instructions, explain your qualifications, and be yourself.

Invitations

Make them personal. Use discreet flattery.

Direct mailshots

Research your target readers, tailor your message to them, and keep the information simple.

➡ CHAPTER 8: ORGANISING YOUR WRITING

Use lists, but make them consistent. Use bullet points, but sparingly.

With reports, or any volume of written information, ask yourself these questions, in order:

- *What is it for?* Check the brief. Make sure you know what you're trying to achieve, and therefore what format is appropriate.
- *Who is it for?* Remember the reader – unlike most instruction manuals! If in doubt, assume total ignorance. Tailor the form and language appropriately.
- *What should it say?* Try writing a summary at this stage – it should help you to concentrate on what your report is really trying to say. Use highlighter pens to organise each subject heading. Create a logical structure.
- *How should it say it?* Write your first draft: title, contents list, summary, introduction/objectives/terms of reference, body of report, conclusions/recommendations, appendices.
- *How does it look, and does it read well?* Leave it overnight. Get a second opinion. Check for jargon and technical language. Check for look: can you make it more appealing?

Finally, make sure it goes to the right people. Write covering letters if necessary.

➡ CHAPTER 9: ELECTRONIC MAIL

Electronic mail (e-mail) is a fact of life for over 55 million people in the world. It's quick and convenient and has many advantages:

- It's spontaneous and tends to reflect immediate thoughts.

- It goes anywhere in the world for the cost of a local call.
- It cuts out the risks of interruption.
- It reduces the need for meetings.
- It saves time and money.

E-mail is developing a language and convention of its own. 'Smileys' are now commonly used to express the writer's feelings, symbols made up of dots, dashes and brackets to indicate the state of mind of the writer. Happy? :-) Sad? :-(And a multitude of others.

It's an informal medium that encourages easy communication and gossip. There is often none of the conventional tools of font enhancements (italic, bold, underline etc.), margins and spell-checkers, each of which get in the way of spontaneity; and it's a great way of getting in touch with colleagues and friends overseas.

Many people use e-mail with little regard for the traditional conventions of writing. Yet it is increasingly being used by businesses to promote goods and services to potential clients. The danger is that it's *so* easy to be spontaneous, you forget to read what you've written before you click the send button – and once it's gone, it's gone.

Yet there's no reason why e-mail communications should be different from any other sort of writing. So:

- Apply the principles of good writing.
- Be as brief as possible.
- Use a tone appropriate for the reader.
- Be clear.

Don't use e-mail for long communications or for confidential documents. You never know where your message could end up!

➡ CHAPTER 10: CORPORATE WRITING DISEASE

Corporate Writing Disease (CWD) is a malady suffered by many businesses. It manifests itself as:

- pomposity

- verbosity
- tautology
- obfuscation
- nounitis
- jargon

Don't waffle. Writers of corporate documents have a tendency to duplicate the language they use in their day-to-day dealings with colleagues. Sitting round a boardroom table discussing the detail of your business with other experts is one thing; using that language in literature meant to appeal to the outside world is another.

Don't overuse nouns to sound extra impressive. Keep a good balance between the number of nouns and the number of verbs. And don't exaggerate by doubling up on descriptive words.

There's no single style of CWD – all organisations and institutions have their own language and jargon. But when you want to promote your work, don't get caught up in management-speak. Remember that most of your readers appreciate simple words and phrases.

All the average reader wants is a well reasoned, clear document to which they can relate. Just remember – keep your words as simple as possible. Clarity is the soul of comprehension.

➡ CONCLUSIONS

The aim of *Business Writing* is to help you write professional, effective, readable documents – whether they be memos, faxes, e-mails, reports or articles. A few bullet points sum up the book's message:

- Understanding your readers is the key to your success – listen to them, find out what they want, and then write for them.
- Use simple, active language – avoid jargon, abstract nouns, and management-speak.
- Listen to what you write – think of your writing as conversation.
- Learn the tricks of the trade – grammar and punctuation – and

use them effectively.
- Organise your writing – start with the message, promote the key ideas, then build up the rest of the content.
- Make sure what you have written is easy on the eye.

Above all, write with purpose – it will make all the difference.

Index

abstractions 15–16, 116–17
active voice 12–15
addresses
 e-mail 103–5
 letters 38, 48, 49–50
adjectives 12, 29
adverbs 12
advertising 78–81, 128
Aitken, Gillon 28
Amnesty International 86
annual reports 91, 93, 96
apologies, written 59,61–3, 112, 126
apostrophes 30–1
appendices 91, 99
application letters 54–6,125–6
Arial (font) 36
articles 12
attachments 106–7
attention span 74, 98
audience, catering for 7–9,47–8, 85–6, 94–6, 101, 122

bad news, explanation 72–3
banks
 CWD 112–13, 118
 loan applications 54–5, 56
baronets 49
bills, chasing 58

bishops 49
bold text 37, 124
Book Antiqua (font) 36
book clubs 87
Bookman Old Style (font) 36
brackets (parentheses) 26, 28, 31–2
building societies, CWD 112
bullet points 90–1

capital letters
 colons 27
 text enhancement 36–7, 124
Century Gothic (font) 36
charities 58–9, 66–7
Churchill, Winston 91–2
clarification, written 72–3, 127
clauses 20
collective nouns 16–17
colons 27
column width 34–5, 124
commas 25–7, 28, 30, 38,48
compassion fatigue 58–9
competence 1
complaints 59–61, 126
concise writing 2, 5–6, 48, 85–6, 91–2
conclusions, report writing 99
conditionals 19
conjunctions 12

contents lists, report writing 98
conversational communication style
  e-mail 107–10, 129–30
  letter openings 51–2
  punctuation 22–4, 122–3
Corporate Writing Disease (CWD) 111–20, 131–2

dashes 27, 28–9
dates 49
deal-clinchers 77
definite articles 12
diagrams 41–2, 95
direct mailshots 85–7, 129
dismissals 67–70, 127

e-mail 102–10, 129–30
  advantages 102–3
  creating messages 103–7
  effective messages 107–10
  perils 109–10
  spam 65
electronic address books 103–5
electronic mail *see* e-mail
enhancement, textual 36–7, 78, 96–7, 124
Esq 48
Eudora 104, 106
evasive communication style 1, 14–16
exaggeration 117–18
exclamation marks 31
executive summaries 96, 98
explanations
  colons 27
  written 72–3, 127
Eyre, Sir Richard 28

Faulks, Sebastian 28
faxes
  of complaint 59–61
  of introduction 65
  layout 38–9
  openings 48–52
  signing off 52–3
feasibility studies 91, 93
flattery 83–5
fliers 75–6
fonts 35–6
forms of communication 47–8, 74, 124–5
Fowler's *Modern English Usage* 24
full stops 24–5, 26
fund-raising 58–9, 66–7
future tense 18–19

gardeners 77–8
Gardner, James 6
Gill (font) 36
grammar 10–21, 122
  howlers 16–21
  positive writing 12–16
  sentence construction 10–12
graphs 41, 42, 95

hairdressers 76–7
Hansard's parliamentary reports 93
Harvard Business Review 32
headers, e-mail 105
headings, letters 50–1
Helvetica (font) 36
highlighter pens 96–7
hyphens 29

I, correct use of 17
impersonal communication 15–16, 49
indefinite articles 12
informal communication, e-mail 107–10, 129–30
information, organisation 89–101, 129
instructions 91
  CWD 113
  layout 42
  target audiences 94–5
insurance companies
  catering for readers 8–9
  direct mailshots 85–6

intensive pronouns 17–18
Internet *see* e-mail
introductions
  letters of 63–5, 126–7
  report writing 97, 98–9
inverted commas 29–30
Investor's Monthly (publication) 6
invitations 82–5, 128
invoices 57, 58
italics 37, 124
its/it's 31

jargon 100, 118–20, 131
jobs
  advertisements 80–1
  applications 81–2, 128
  rejections 70–1
journalists 6, 121
junk mail 65
justification 36, 37–8

knights 49

lateness, dealing with 68–70
layout 33–43, 95, 100, 123–4
leading (line spacing) 35,124
leaflets 75–6
letter writing
  see also e-mail
  apologies 59, 61–3, 112, 126
  applications 54–6, 125–6
  clarifications 72–3, 127
  complaints 59–61, 126
  content 54–73, 125–7
  dismissals 67–70, 127
  explanations 72–3, 127
  introductions 63–5, 126–7
  layouts 37–8
  openings 48–52
  references 65–7, 126–7
  rejections 70–1, 127
  requests 54, 56–9, 125–6
  resignations 71–2, 127
  sales pitches 76–8, 85–7
  signing off 52–3

  warning 67–70, 127
letters
  capital 27, 36–7, 124
  missing 31
line spacing (leading) 35, 124
lists 89–91
  contents 98
  punctuation 27, 28
  request letters 56–7
loans 54–5, 56
local government, CWD 113
logos 37

mailshots, direct 85–7, 129
management summaries 96, 98
management-speak *see* Corporate
  Writing Disease
manuals 91
  CWD 113
  layout 42
  target audiences 94–5
margins 35, 109–10
marketing 74–88, 127–29
  advertising 78–81, 128
  aims 87–8, 128
  direct mailshots 85–7, 129
  invitations 82–5, 128
  job applications 81–2, 128
me, correct use of 17
meaning
  commas 26–7
  modifiers 20–1
meeting reports 91, 93
membership organisations
  applications 55–6
  resignations 71–2
memos
  layout 38
  lucidity 6–7
  openings 48–52
  signing off 52–3
message headers, e-mail 105
messages, effective communication
  5–7, 48, 74, 85–6, 121, 128
minutes 91, 93

mistakes
  CWD 111–20, 130–1
  grammatical 16–21
  modifiers 20–1
  money requests 57, 58–9
  Morris, Bill 32
  music clubs 86–7

names 30–1, 39, 48–9
Natural Environment Research
  Council (NERC) 13
NHS circulars 111–12
nounitis 13, 16, 116–17, 131
nouns
  abstract 15–16, 116–17
  collective 16–17
  definition 12
  hyphens 29
numbers, missing 31

object
  pronouns 17
  sentence construction 11, 12
objectives, report writing 98–9
openings 48–52
organisation, written material
  89–101, 129

paper-clip systems 106–7
paragraphs, numbering 97
parentheses (brackets) 26, 28, 31–2
parliamentary reports 93
Pascal, Blaise 2
passive voice 13–14, 15
past tense 18–20
peers 49
personal touches 67, 83, 122
photocopier engineers 75–6
pie charts 42
plurals
  apostrophes 30
  subject/verb agreement 16–17
positive writing 12–16
possesive pronouns 18
possession, indication of 18, 30–1

postscripts (PS) 52–3
prepositions 12
present perfect tense 19
present tense 18–20
presentation, written 33–43, 95,
  100, 123–4
progress reports 91, 93
pronouns 12, 17–18, 122
PS (postscripts) 52–3
punctuation 22–32, 122–3
purpose of communication 47–8,
  124–5

question marks 31
quotations 27, 29–30, 37

re 50
readers, catering for 7–9, 47–8,
  85–6, 94–6, 101, 122
recommendations, report writing
  99
references 65–7, 126–7
reflexive pronouns 17–18
rejections, written 70–1, 127
reliability, e-mail 110
repetition 114–15
report writing 91–101, 129
  content 96–7
  double checks 100–1
  layout 40–1
  purpose 92–3
  readers 94–6
  structure 97–9
reporters 6, 121
requests 54, 56–9, 125–6
research reports 93, 95
resignations 72, 127
responsibility, evasion 14
Roddick, Anita 28
royalty 49
Russell, Lord Earl 49

sales 74–88, 127–29
  advertising 78–81, 128
  aims 87–8, 128

direct mailshots 85-7, 129
invitations 82-5, 128
job applications 81-2, 128
proposals 91, 94
sans-serif typefaces 36,37
security, e-mail 110
semi-colons 27-8
sentences
  construction 10-12, 122
  grammar 10-21
  length 11, 122
  meaning 20-1, 26-7
  punctuation 24-32
serifs 36, 37
signing off 52-3
singular, subject/verb agreement 16-17
Smileys 110, 129
spam 65
subject
  modifiers 21
  pronouns 17
  sentence construction 11-12
  verb agreement 16-17
subject lines, e-mail 106-7
summaries, report writing 96, 98, 129

tables 40-1, 95
tautology 114-15
tenses 18-20
terms of reference 98-9
Thatcher, Margaret 29
Times New Roman (font) 36
titles
  personal 48-9
  report writing 97-8, 100
tone of communication 47-8
trade associations, applications 55-6
type style 35-6, 37, 124

underlined text 37, 124
unique selling point (USP) 74
Univers (font) 36
urgency, effective communication 7
USP *see* unique selling point

verbosity 114-16
verbs
  active 14-15
  definition 11, 12
  list construction 90-1
  sentence construction 11,13
  subject agreement 16-17
waffle 2, 5-6, 48, 51-2,91-2, 114-16, 131
warning letters 67-70, 127
word processors 33, 35-6

Courses and Workshops

For open courses or tailor-made workshops in effective business writing, contact

Clarity

business solutions – in writing

Also specialising in

- speeches
- reports
- ghost-writing

Call

07000 4 WORDS

(07000 496 737)

or contact **Clarity** at
6 Adam Street, London WC2N 6AA

Tel 0171 379 8812
Fax 0171 497 1441
e-mail sally@clarity4words.co.uk
web site www.clarity4words.co.uk